CAMBRIDGE
Primary English

Workbook 2

Gill Budgell & Kate Ruttle

T0159704

CAMBRIDGE
UNIVERSITY PRESS

University Printing House, Cambridge CB2 8BS, United Kingdom

One Liberty Plaza, 20th Floor, New York, NY 10006, USA

477 Williamstown Road, Port Melbourne, VIC 3207, Australia

314–321, 3rd Floor, Plot 3, Splendor Forum, Jasola District Centre, New Delhi – 110025, India

103 Penang Road, #05-06/07, Visioncrest Commercial, Singapore 238467

Cambridge University Press is part of the University of Cambridge.

It furthers the University's mission by disseminating knowledge in the pursuit of education, learning and research at the highest international levels of excellence.

www.cambridge.org
Information on this title: www.cambridge.org/9781108789943

First published 2015
Second edition 2021

20 19 18 17 16 15 14 13 12 11 10 9

Printed in Italy by L.E.G.O. S.p.A.

A catalogue record for this publication is available from the British Library

ISBN 978-1-108-78994-3 Paperback with Digital Access (1 Year)

Cambridge University Press has no responsibility for the persistence or accuracy of URLs for external or third-party internet websites referred to in this publication, and does not guarantee that any content on such websites is, or will remain, accurate or appropriate. Information regarding prices, travel timetables, and other factual information given in this work is correct at the time of first printing but Cambridge University Press does not guarantee the accuracy of such information thereafter.

....

....

Contents

How to use this book

This workbook provides questions for you to practise what you have learned in class. There is a unit to match each unit in your Learner's Book. There are six or twelve sessions in each unit and each session is divided into three parts:

Focus: these questions help you to master the basics ⟶

Practice: these questions help you to become more confident in using what you have learned ⟶

Challenge: these questions will make you think more deeply ⟶

Focus

1 a How many letters are in these words?

friends		photographs	
families		class	

b Which words have three claps or syllables? Underline them in the chart.

c Which word begins with a **digraph**? Circle it.

d Write in the missing letter at the end of these words.

famil_   happ_   fl_

e Which word above is the odd one out? Why?

The odd word out is _____ because _____

Practice

2 a How many letters are in these words?

million		brain	
approximately		heart	

Challenge

3 Write these sentences again using speech marks and the correct punctuation.

Add who is saying each sentence.
It doesn't have to be Daisy or Mum.

Try to use a another verb for 'said' each time.

1 > Friends and families

> 1.1 Friends at school

Focus

1 a How many letters are in these words?

friends		photographs	
families		class	

b Which words have three claps or syllables?
   <u>Underline</u> them in the chart.

c Which word begins with a **digraph**? Circle it.

d Write in the missing letter at the end of these words.

   famil_   happ_   fl_

e Which word above is the odd one out? Why?

   The odd word out is _____ because _____

   _____ .

Practice

2 a How many letters are in these words?

million		brain	
approximately		heart	

b Which words have the same number of claps or syllables?
   <u>Underline</u> them in the chart above.

c What is the same in each of these words?
   Circle the patterns.

madam	photograph	kayak

Challenge

3 Write four quiz questions for a
   partner to answer.

Write a word
in four boxes as
in 2a above.

Speaking tip

use the quiz above for ideas.

a How many letters are in these words?

My quiz

b Which words have ___ claps or syllables? <u>Underline</u> them.

My quiz

c Which words have three letters but one sound? Circle the words.

My quiz

d Which word is the odd one out? Why?

My quiz

The odd word out is _____ because _____

_____ .

⟩ 1.2 A family adventure

Focus

Letters at the beginning and end can change the meanings of words.

1 Join the opposites. <u>Underline</u> the word beginnings.

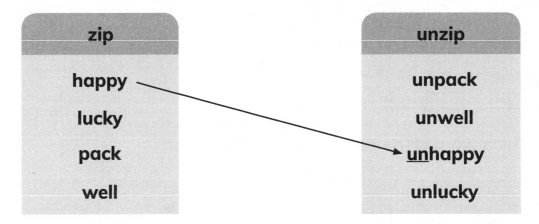

zip
happy
lucky
pack
well

unzip
unpack
unwell
<u>un</u>happy
unlucky

Practice

2 Add the letters –ly to the end of the underlined words to make a new sentence.

a Mr and Mrs Chen were tired from working all day. It was <u>normal</u>.

Mr and Mrs Chen were

_____ tired from working all day.

b The lights went out. It was <u>sudden</u>.

_____, the lights went out.

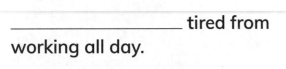

Adding the ending -ly to a word can change the kind of word it is.

c 'Wow! It's so dark in here,' said Ben. He was <u>excited</u>.

   'Wow! It's so dark in here,' said Ben _____ .

d It was just <u>luck</u> that Dad found a torch.

   _____, Dad found a torch.

e 'I can fix the problem of Grandma's melting ice cream cake,' said Ben.
   He was <u>helpful</u>.

   _____

   _____

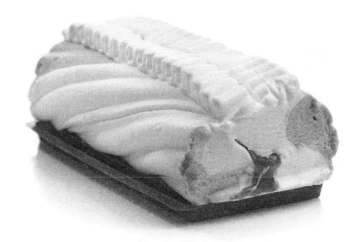

Challenge

Letters at the beginning and ending of words can change
the meanings of words.

3 Look at the chart on the next page.

   a Draw lines in one colour to join each word beginning
      or ending to its word and sentence.

   b Draw lines in another colour to join each word
      beginning or ending to its meaning.

Word and sentence	Word beginnings and endings	Meaning
wonderful It was a wonderful adventure.	un–	'none' or 'not'
useless The torch was useless without batteries.	re–	'not' or the opposite of the rest of the word
unusual It was an unusual evening.	–ful	'again'
recharge Amy had recharged her tablet.	–less	'a lot of'

c Write another word for each for these word beginnings and endings.

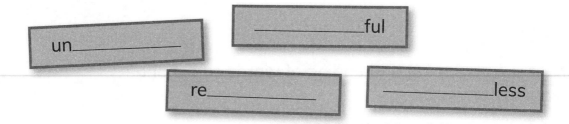

un_____

_____ful

re_____

_____less

> 1.3 Retelling and acting

Focus

1 Fill in the gaps. Use the words in the boxes to help you.

too   to   only   the   off

a It was an evening just like any other in _____ Chen family apartment.

b Suddenly, the lights went _____ . It was a power cut.

c Mr Chen found his torch, but it was _____ a small beam.

d The apartment got hot and the fridge and freezer stopped working _____ .

e Grandma's ice cream cake was going _____ melt.

Practice

2 Fill the gaps with missing verbs.

a 'Is everybody okay?' _____ Mr Chen.

b Amy _____ a good idea to use the light from her tablet.

c Ben had a good idea to eat the ice cream cake before it _____ .

d Later, the power _____ back on.

e Then the problem was how to tell Grandma that they had

_____ her cake.

Challenge

3 Fill the gaps with nouns or noun phrases including adjectives.

a It was an evening _____ .

b Mr and Mrs Chen were _____ from work and the children were

_____ playing on tablets.

c Suddenly, the lights went off. The apartment was _____ .

d There was only a _____ from the torch.

e The _____ will melt if it gets warm.

> 1.4 Describing what characters do

Language focus

I collect bottle tops, toilet roll holders, insects and bits of rock.

Remember that this is a **comma,**

It tells us to take a short pause when we are reading.

We can use it to separate items in a list.

We need to put 'and' between the last two items in a list.

Focus

Don't add a comma if there are only two things in a list.

1 Tick ✓ the sentences that have commas in the correct place. Correct the others.

a I have an older brother, a younger brother and a sister. ☐

b We searched all day for, sticks, stones, and shells. ☐

c The box was full of feathers pebbles and, seeds. ☐

d I have an old collection of toy cars, vans, lorries and garages. ☐

Practice

2 Use the words in the list to complete the sentences. Add commas and 'and' in the right places.

a I collect _____ .

stamps   dolls   joke books

b On the school trip I was in a group with _____

_____ .

Anish   Zoe   Paulo   Ann

c At the zoo I saw _____ .

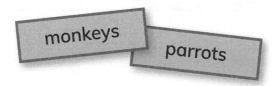

monkeys   parrots

d   I have a collection of small things like _____

_____ .

coins

gems

petals

shells

Challenge

3   Rewrite the sentences using commas and 'and' in the correct places.

a In my family I have a mum and a dad and a brother and a sister.	
b Beno and Omar and Hamidi and Zayan are my best friends at school.	
c My younger sister collects bugs and leaves and twigs.	
d I collect games and quiz cards and jokes.	
e I can make origami fish and swans and frogs and boats.	

> 1.5 Challenges and excuses

Language focus

We can use **verbs ending in –ing** to talk about things that are happening now.

We can use **verbs ending in –ed** to talk about things that happened in the past.

Verb	–ing	–ed
check	He is checking.	He checked.

Be careful: some verbs are irregular!

fly	*He is flying.*	*He flew.*

Focus

1 Fill in the gaps with verbs ending in –ed or –ing.

Everything used to be peaceful. But then one day I got a great idea.

I was _____ and I could see the sand pile almost under me.

I _____ to make sure there were no trucks in it.

Then I _____ off from the swing. It was like _____ .

There was a minute when I was sitting still in the air and then it was like

parachuting. I _____ in the sand pile.

Practice

2 a Fill in the gaps with verbs ending in –ed or –ing. Use these words to help you. They are different from the verbs in the story.

b Draw a picture in each box.

tied wasted needed making jumped wanted

It was Huey's turn.

1 He _____ to put on his baseball cap.

2 He _____ his lucky shirt.

3 He was _____ excuses.

4 He _____ his shoe laces.

5 He _____ down from the swing.

6 He had _____ his turn.

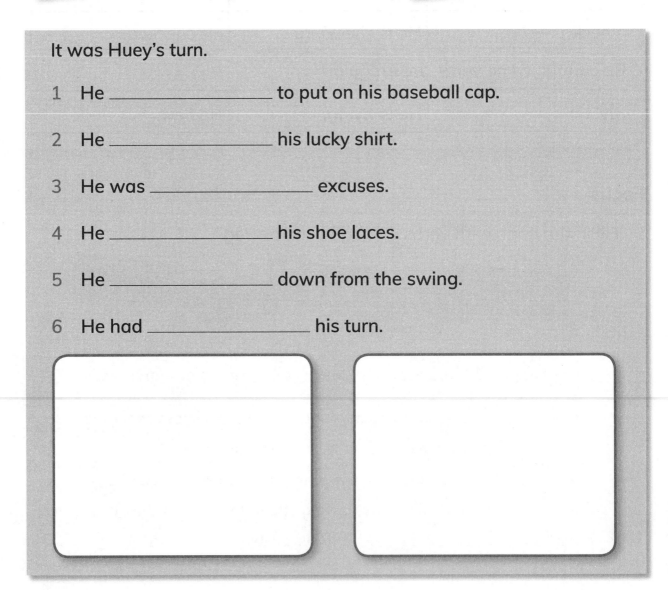

Challenge

3 a Replace each underlined verb with a different one ending in –ed or –ing.

b Draw a picture in each box.

- Everything used to be peaceful. But then one day I <u>got</u> _____ a great idea.

- I was swinging and I could see the sand pile almost under me. I <u>checked</u> _____ to make sure there were no trucks in it.

- Then I <u>pushed off</u> _____ from the swing.

- It was like flying. There was a minute when I was <u>sitting</u> _____ still in the air

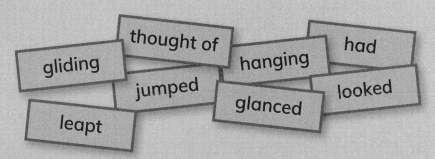

- And then it was like <u>parachuting</u> _____ . I landed in the sand pile.

- "All right!" Gloria said. She got in the swing. In a minute she <u>flew</u> _____ too, just like me.

- "Your turn, Huey!" I said.

- "OK," Huey <u>said</u> _____ . He didn't sound very excited.

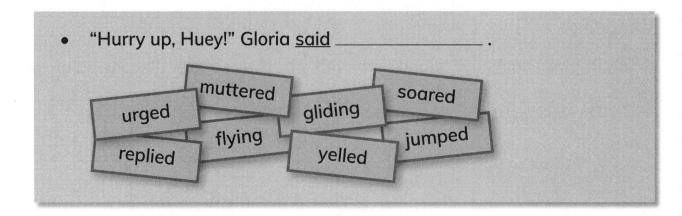

- "Hurry up, Huey!" Gloria <u>said</u> _____ .

muttered   soared   urged   gliding   flying   replied   yelled   jumped

> 1.6 Brother trouble

Focus

1 a Tick ✓ the things Julian's father put into the lemon pudding.

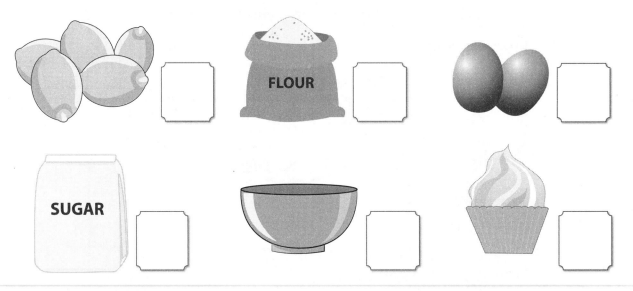

FLOUR

SUGAR

b Draw your favourite pudding and write what you put in it.

Practice

2 Write an A–Z of puddings. Finish writing the letters of the alphabet first.
Then think of a pudding name that has a word beginning with each letter.

A for apple pudding	B	C	D
E			
	J for jungle jam pudding		
		O	
Q			
			X
	Z		

Challenge

3 Sort these puddings into alphabetical order. Number them 1–8.

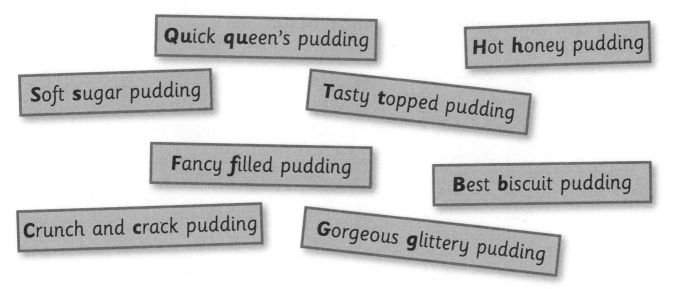

Quick queen's pudding

Hot honey pudding

Soft sugar pudding

Tasty topped pudding

Fancy filled pudding

Best biscuit pudding

Crunch and crack pudding

Gorgeous glittery pudding

> 1.7 Sequencing and adding to a story

Focus

1 Sort the sentences into the correct order. Write a number to show the order.

a Huey and Julian guarded the pudding. ☐

b Father took a nap. ☐

c Huey tasted the pudding and then so did I! ☐

d Father made a pudding – a wonderful pudding! ☐

e Huey and Julian helped him make it. ☐

Practice

2 Sort the words into the correct order.
Write the sentence and add the correct punctuation.

a are you make going to what

_____

b will like it taste a whole lemons of raft

_____

c squirted my in eye juice

_____

Challenge

3 Sort the letters into the correct order to spell the word.
The first letter of the word is underlined.

ddiu<u>p</u>ng   <u>k</u>chinte

queeedz<u>s</u>   onme<u>l</u>

_____   _____

_____   _____

4 Write a sentence for each word.

_____

_____

_____

_____

> 1.8 Describing what characters say

Focus

1 Label these sentences and phrases.
Write **S** for a statement or **Q** for a question.

a Why can I never find my keys? _____

b Close your mouth and eat your food. _____

c Will you listen to me, please? _____

2 In your reading book, find an example of these things.
Write the example in the space.

a a statement or sentence

_____

b a question

_____

> **Language focus**
>
> Remember, we use a **full stop** at the end of a sentence or statement. **.**
> We use a **question mark** at the end of a question. **?**

Practice

3 Add the punctuation to each of these sentences and phrases.

   a Did you hear what I said

   b Don't stare, it's rude

   c I won't tell you again

   d Why do you not listen

4 Write an example of your own.

   a a statement or sentence

   _____

   b a question

   _____

Challenge

5 Add all the missing punctuation to each of these sentences and phrases.

   a shall I write it down for you

   b this is a wonderful gift

   c how did you know

   d put all your stuff away now please

   e don t whisper its rude

> 1.9 Mum and daughter fun

> **Language focus**
>
> **Speech marks** look like this " . . . " or this ' . . . '.
> They show when someone starts and stops speaking.

Focus

1 Add the speech marks for these sentences.

   a Eat your peas, said Mum.

   b I don't like peas, said Daisy.

   c If you eat your peas, you can have some pudding, Mum said.

   d I like green beans, Daisy said.

Practice

2 Look at the chart. Add speech marks to the sentences in the boxes.

Daisy speech	Mum speech
"I don't like anything green," said Daisy.	Hurry up and eat your peas, Daisy! shouted Mum.
Daisy said, I don't like the taste of green vegetables!	Mum asked, What do you like?

Challenge

3 Write these sentences again using speech marks and the correct punctuation.

Add who is saying each sentence.
It doesn't have to be Daisy or Mum.

Try to use a another verb for 'said' each time.

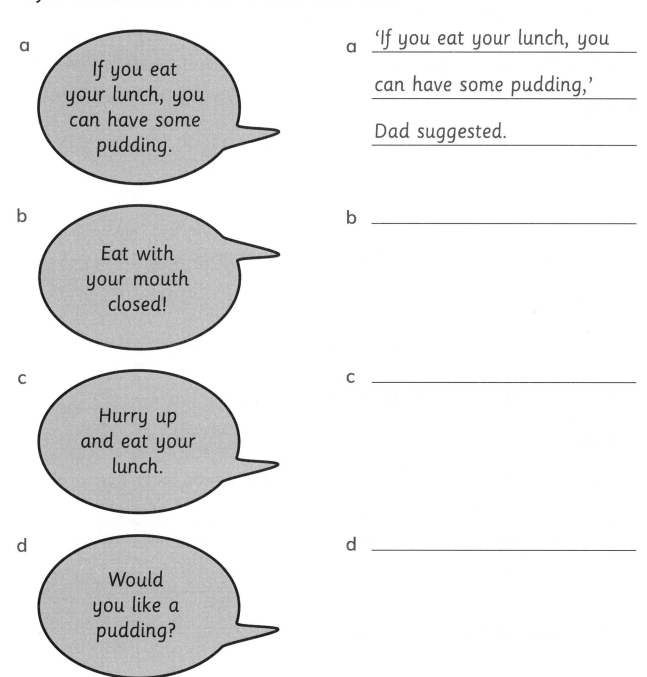

a

If you eat your lunch, you can have some pudding.

a 'If you eat your lunch, you

can have some pudding,'

Dad suggested.

b

Eat with your mouth closed!

b _____

c

Hurry up and eat your lunch.

c _____

d

Would you like a pudding?

d _____

> 1.10 Exploring language

> **Language focus**
>
> We use these words when we talk about the number of something:
> **how much** or **how many.**
>
> We can use: all   some   more   a lot of
>
>   no   any   most   lots of

Focus

1 Read these sentences. <u>Underline</u> words that tell you *how much*
   or *how many*.

   a There are lots of things I like eating.

   b I ate some olives but I didn't like the black ones.

   c We don't have any ice cream at home.

   d There are no vegetables on my plate.

   e I have got more sweets than you.

Practice

2 Answer these quiz questions. Use one of the words in the box
   above in each answer.

   a How much milk do you drink?

   _____

   b Do you eat more vegetables or more fruit?

   _____

c   If you had a chocolate bar, how much would you eat?

_____

d   If you have a bag of sweets, how many do you share?

_____

e   What would you eat a lot of?

_____

Challenge

3   Fold and cut a piece of paper into six pieces.
    Write a number on each piece of paper 1-6.
    Put the number cards in a bag. Mix them up.

4   Pick a number card.

> **Tip**
>
> Put the number card back in the bag and mix the cards up each time.

a   Write a sentence for that number.

If you pick	Write a sentence using:	Write your sentence
1	all	
2	more	
3	most	
4	lots of	
5	no	
6	any	

b   Keep picking until you have a sentence for all the numbers.

> 1.11 Planning and writing a funny family story

Focus

1 Fill the gaps using one of these words.

a You can eat some pudding _____ stay up for an extra hour.

b You don't have to wash _____ brush your teeth.

c You can have anything you like _____ you must eat your peas.

d Mum wants Daisy to eat her peas _____ she does not like brussel sprouts.

Practice

2 Write one sentence for each pair using the words above in Focus.

a I'll buy every supermarket. I'll buy every sweetshop.

_____

b You never have to go to bed again. You never have to go to school.

_____

c I will buy you anything you want. I want you to eat your peas.

_____

d I do want all those things. I don't like peas.

_____

Challenge

3 Write your own sentences using these words.

and   _____

but   _____

if   _____

because   _____

› 1.12 Look back

Focus

1 Choose a piece of your own story writing.

a Re-read your writing to check for mistakes, to see what is good and what you can improve.

b Fill in the chart.

	What is good?	Why is it good?	What can you improve?
What you think			

Practice

2 a Ask a partner to read the same piece of writing.
Then ask for their feedback.

Fill in this chart.

	What is good?	Why is it good?	What can you improve?
What others think			

b Highlight what you will try to do next time.

Challenge

3 Find a story about family life you would like to read.
Look at home, in the school library or online.

4 Draw a picture of the story here and say why you want to read it.
How could it help you to improve your own reading and writing?

2 > Badges

> 2.1 Instructions everywhere

Focus

1 Draw an instruction.

2 Write an instruction.

_____

_____

Practice

3 Look at these instructions.

What is each instruction telling you to do or not to do?
Write a sentence about each instruction.

Instruction a:

_____

Instruction b:

_____

Instruction c:

_____

Instruction d:

_____

Writing tip

Remember to use a capital letter at the beginning of your
instruction and a full stop at the end. You may want to use
the word and to join two parts of a sentence together.

Challenge

4   Write three instructions or top tips for helping someone to work
    well with a partner. Think about the features you will use.

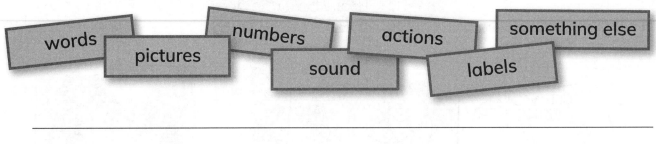

_____

_____

_____

› 2.2 Listening to, and reading, instructions

Focus

1 Read the text about scientists.

What is a scientist?

What do scientists do?

Scientists try to find out new things about the world around us by doing experiments.

What is an experiment?

An experiment is when you do something to find out what happens. You usually need to ask questions and write or follow instructions.

Can I be a scientist?

Yes! If you are interested in asking questions and then finding a way to work out the answers then you can be a scientist too.
You have to be able to write and follow instructions.

2 Fill in this chart.

Word	How many syllables?	How many times can you find the words in the text?
find		
science		
scientist(s)		
experiment(s)		

Practice

3 a Fill in the chart using words from the text above.

Number of syllables	Word(s)
1	
2	
3	
4	
5	
6	

b Are there any columns without words in them?
Find a word that links to science to fill it. Where will you look?

Challenge

4 Change the number of syllables in each word by adding word beginnings or endings. Use each word beginning or ending once. Write the number of syllables the new word has.

> You may have to change the spelling of some words when you add the extra syllable. My best example is syllable – syllabification! Can you say that?

Word beginning	Word	Word ending	Longer word	Number of syllables
re–	instruct	–ly		
	equip			
dis–	confident	–ment		
	organise			
un–	appear	–ion	instruction	3
	seen			

> 2.3 Commands for instructing

> **Language focus**
>
> Features of **instructional texts**:
>
> - They often have a heading that begins: *How to ...* .
> - They may give us steps, rules or tips to follow.
> - The main points may be in a bulleted list.
> - They may have pictures or photographs.
> - They begin with a command.
>   A command is a word that tells us what to do: *Check ...* , *Be ...* .

Focus

1 Look at each picture. Say what it is about. Tick (✓) the best heading.

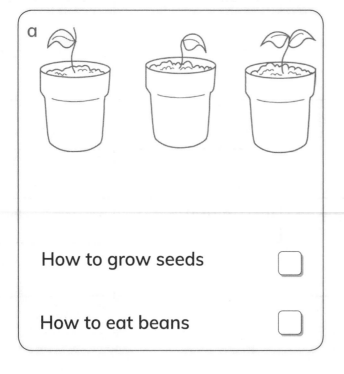

How to grow seeds ☐

How to eat beans ☐

How to make a hand puppet ☐

How to make a shadow ☐

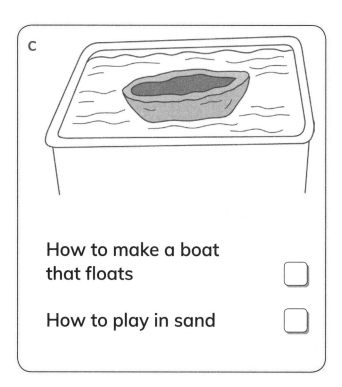

c

How to make a boat that floats ☐

How to play in sand ☐

d

How to make dirty coins shiny ☐

How to save pocket money ☐

Practice

2 a Number the instructions to show the correct order.

<u>How to make dirty coins shiny</u>

Take out your coins and clean them. ☐

The coins will look new and shiny. ☐

Tip a little of the ketchup or vinegar into a bowl. ☐

Get some tomato ketchup or vinegar. ☐

Soak your coins overnight. ☐

b What question do you want to ask about this experiment?

_____

_____

Challenge

Write a statement for four of the headings from Activity 1.

Begin with one of these words. They are adverbs of time:

3 Write a statement for each of the four picture headings in the Focus activity.

Begin your statement with one of these words.

One has been done for you.

Example: *How to grow seeds.*

> always   sometimes   never

Never forget to water your seeds.

_____

_____

_____

_____

_____

_____

_____

_____

> 2.4 Reading and following instructions 1

> **Language focus**
>
> Even in a flow chart we use **correct sentence punctuation**.
> Statements, commands and questions all need correct punctuation too.
>
> Remember, we use a capital letter to begin a sentence.
> We end a sentence with a full stop (.) or a question mark (?)

Focus

1   Add **six** full stops to this text. Write a capital letter after each
    full stop you add. An example has been done for you.

How to blow bubbles is an instructional text. It tells you about
how you can blow bubbles each sentence adds new information
to what you knew before so you have to read the text in order
the text is in a chart and uses instruction verbs it has arrows to
help you to understand the writing it makes the instructions clear
but more fun too you should read the text so you know how to
blow bubbles

Practice

2   Rewrite each sentence with the correct punctuation.

a   what do scientists do

    _____

b   It is amazing to see the bubbles

    _____

c why not try the experiment if you have time

_____

d do the instructions work

_____

e write a list of equipment

_____

f how do you make a bubble painting

_____

Challenge

3 Write these sentences as two simple sentences.
Make the punctuation changes that you need.
An example has been done for you.

a You need a bowl and you need a jug of water.

_You need a bowl. You need a jug of water._____

b You need oil and you need some washing-up liquid.

_____

c You need a spoon, but you do not need a fork.

_____

d Check your equipment and then pour some water into the bowl.

_____

e Add some cooking oil and then add some washing-up liquid.

_____

f Add some washing-up liquid, but only add a few drops.

_____

› 2.5 Numbers for ordering

Focus

1 Choose from the words below to fill the gap in each sentence.

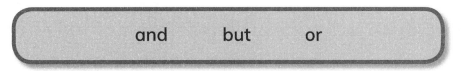

and   but   or

a Observe things in detail _____ ask lots of questions.

b Ask questions _____ listen carefully too.

c Follow instructions _____ work out what you have to do to answer your question.

d Record your results _____ discuss them with your group.

e Use your senses to explore _____ never take risks.

Practice

2 Choose from the words below to fill the gap in each sentence.

> because   so   although

a We listened carefully _____ we understood what to do.

b _____ we listened carefully we were not sure what to do.

c We knew what to do _____ we talked about it afterwards.

d The experiment worked _____ we worked together.

e We enjoyed it _____ it was quite difficult.

Challenge

3 Use the words from Activity 1 or Activity 2 to rewrite these pairs of sentences as one sentence.

a We enjoy science. We really enjoy exciting experiments.

_____

b She wants to be the leader. She talks too much.

_____

c Our experiment did not work. We did not work well together.

_____

d We do science every week. We sometimes have to do geography too.

_____

e We look after the equipment. Others can do the experiment next time.

_____

› 2.6 Reading and following instructions 2

Focus

1 Read the sentences. Write the correct verb form in the gap.

a We answer quietly when the teacher _____ us.

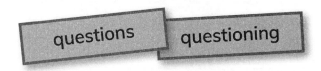

questions   questioning

b They _____ the pizza for us all to share.

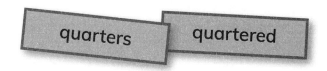

quarters   quartered

c We _____ with fear when we saw the experiment had gone wrong.

quivering   quivered

d We couldn't hear the questions because the ducks were

_____ .

quacks   quacking

e We worked out that 100 and 550 _____ 650.

equalling   equals

Practice

2 a Sort the words into three sets of word endings (–s, –ing or –ed).

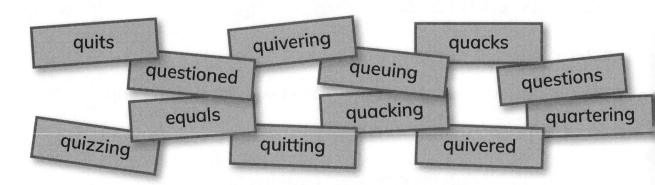

Set 1	Set 2	Set 3

b What word is the odd one out? _____

Challenge

3   Remember the question words: what, when, how, why, who.

Write some questions for a partner to answer.
Use a qu word in each question.

Example:

What is the point of quitting?

_____

_____

_____

_____

> 2.7 Sentence starters

Language focus

These words tell us what to do in what order.
They help us to understand the correct order of the text.
We usually use them at the beginning of a series of sentences.

first   next   finally

Focus

1 Tick (✓) the words that help you to understand order.

☐ and   ☐ next

☐ second   ☐ but

☐ finally   ☐ bubbles

☐ experiment   ☐ then

☐ because   ☐ so

Practice

2 Add the missing words to these instructions.
   These words tell you what to do in the right order.

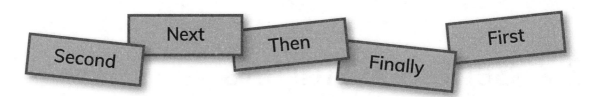

a _____ make sure you have all your equipment.

b _____ pour some water into a bowl.

c _____ add some cooking oil. Observe.

d _____ add some washing-up liquid and stir the water.

e _____ observe. What has changed? Why?

Challenge

3 Write some instructions for how to grow something. Begin each instruction with the words from Activities 1 and 2.

_____

_____

_____

_____

_____

> 2.8 Matching personal information to badges

Language focus

Personal information is information about you. It may include:

- your first name
- your family name
- your age
- your address

- what you look like
- things you like doing
- things you like to eat.

Keep your personal information safe.

Focus

1 Fill in the form with your personal details.

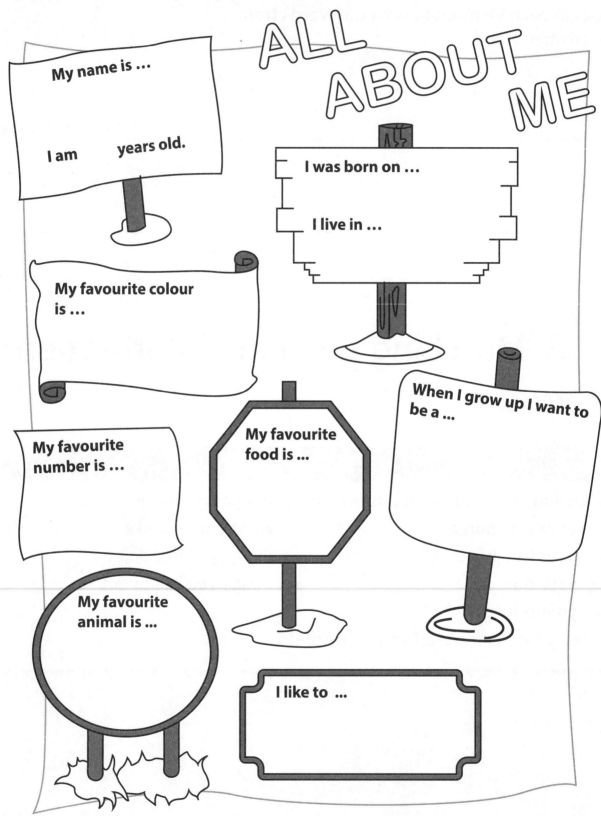

Practice

2 Pretend you are creating a new badge for your school.

a Make notes about what you will include on it and explain why.

_____

_____

_____

_____

_____

b Create your new badge here.

Challenge

3 Pretend you are applying to be a special helper at a school open day for new parents.

You have to give some personal information to the head teacher.

Design your own form for your personal information.
What sort of personal information would be important to include?

> 2.9 Exploring reading choices

Language focus

If we talk about more than one thing, we use **plurals**.

To make a plural we often just add –s to a word.
But there are irregular plurals too.

1 book	2 books	1 quiz	10 quizzes	1 life	lots of lives
1 boy	2 boys	1 story	3 stories	1 child	4 children
1 zoo	city zoos	A superhero	superheroes	A series	hundreds of series

Focus

1   Sort the words into singular nouns and plural nouns. Write two lists.

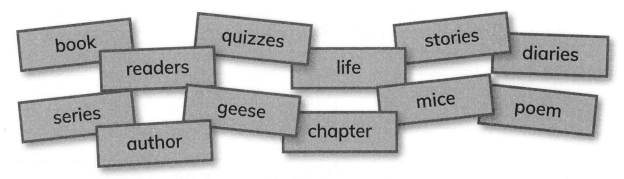

book   quizzes   stories   diaries   readers   life   series   geese   mice   poem   chapter   author

Singular nouns	Plural nouns

Practice

2 Look at the chart. Join each pair of words to its rule.

Singular and plural words		The rule	Another word for this rule
1 book	2 books	Ends in consonant + o, add –es	
1 bus	2 buses	Add –s	
1 leaf	2 leaves	Irregular nouns, no rules	
1 key	2 keys	No change	
1 party	2 parties	Ends in f, add –ves	
1 kangaroo	2 kangaroos	Ends in vowel + y, add –s	
1 tomato	2 tomatoes	Ends in vowel + o, add –s	
1 foot	2 feet	Ends in s, add –es	
1 deer	2 deer	Ends in consonant + y, add –ies	

Challenge

3 Use the chart above. Write another word for each rule in the final column.

› 2.10 Reading about badges

Focus

1 Choose a book you have enjoyed in the last few weeks.

    a Draw the book cover here.

    b Write five quiz questions about it.

_____

_____

_____

_____

_____

Practice

2 Choose a book you have enjoyed in the last month.
Write a book review.

Title and author:

_____

What I liked:

_____

_____

What I disliked:

_____

_____

Something I noticed:

_____

_____

Overall star rating out of 5:

_____

Challenge

A blog is where a writer or group of writers share ideas and opinions about something.

3 Think about designing a class blog
   page for sharing book ideas and
   reviews.

Blog Ideas

a Make a list of what you would
   include in your blog.

_____

_____

_____

_____

_____

b Draw how you might organise the ideas.

> 2.11 Planning and writing a new badge pathway

Focus

1 a Look at the badges. In each set, one badge is the odd one out. Explain why and cross it out.

The odd badge out is the _____ because _____

_____.

The odd badge out is the _____ because _____

_____.

The odd badge out is the _____ because _____

_____.

b Draw your own set of badges with an odd one out in the last line.

Practice

2 Read all of the words. In each line, one word is the odd one out.
Explain why and cross the word out.

a badge   bridge   bandage

The odd word out is _____ because _____

_____.

b pathway   walk   footprint

The odd word out is _____ because _____

_____.

c guide   stage   page

The odd word out is _____ because _____

_____.

d read   writing   spell

The odd word out is _____ because _____

_____.

e first   quick   next

The odd word out is _____ because _____

_____.

Challenge

3   Write an *odd one out* challenge for your partner to complete.

Write five challenges using a mix of pictures, numbers and words.

Challenge 1:

Challenge 2:

Challenge 3:

Challenge 4:

Challenge 5:

Make sure you have an answer sheet before you challenge your partner.

> 2.12 Look back

Focus

1 Think about when you worked in a group.
This could be any work in this unit.

a What did you do well?

b What could you do better next time?

c Fill in this chart.

What went well?	Why did it go well?	What could you improve?

Practice

2 Talk to someone from your group.

a Ask for their feedback on how well you work in a group.

b Fill in this chart. Use a coloured pencil to highlight what you will try to work on.

What I do well in a group	Why I do well	What I can improve

Challenge

3 Think about the best badge pathway. Fill in this chart.

How we decided on the best pathway	Why it won	My view

3 All about sounds

> 3.1 Repeating letter sounds

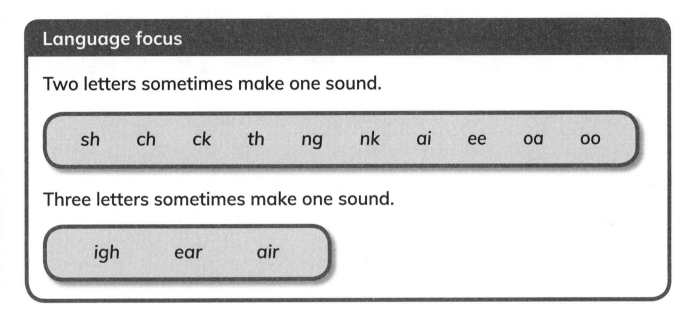

Language focus

Two letters sometimes make one sound.

| sh | ch | ck | th | ng | nk | ai | ee | oa | oo |

Three letters sometimes make one sound.

| igh | ear | air |

Focus

1 Write the missing letters in the poem. Use the letter sets to help you.

| sh | ck | ch |

Shop Chat

My _____op sto_____s: taps, tri_____s,

lo_____s, _____ips,   _____ip's clocks,

_____opsti_____s,   lipsti_____ and _____imney pots.

Wat_____ straps,   What does your _____op stock?

traps, tops,   _____arkskin so_____s.

Practice

2 Write the beginning and end letters to finish these words.
Add a word to each list.

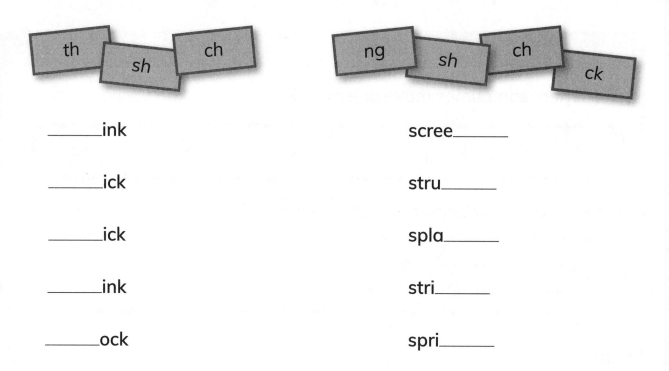

_____ink   scree_____

_____ick   stru_____

_____ick   spla_____

_____ink   stri_____

_____ock   spri_____

Challenge

3 Mark the words with dots to show each letter sound.

Shop Chat

a My shop stocks: f taps, tricks,

b locks, chips,   g ship's clocks,

c chopsticks,   h lipstick **and** chimney
                                   pots.

d watch straps,
                                i What **does your** shop
e traps, **tops,**   stock?

> 3.2 Chants

> **Language focus**
>
> The spacing of letters and **words** can be very important in poems.
> The spacing can make a picture. It can also show a pattern.
> Look at the spacing:
>
> - between letters
> - between words
> - between lines
> - around punctuation marks
> - across the page
> - down the page.

Focus

1 Read and copy the first part of the chant. Focus on your capital letters and then lower case letters. Keep your handwriting neat.

WHAT DO WE WANT   clap clap clap

_____

WHAT DO WE LIKE   clap clap clap

_____

WHAT DO WE LOVE   clap clap clap

_____

Practice

2   Read and copy this short chant.
     Focus on your capital letters and then lower case letters.
     Copy the added punctuation marks carefully.
     Keep your handwriting neat and well-spaced.

GIVE US AN	F	clap clap clap

_____

GIVE US A	U	clap clap clap

_____

GIVE US AN	N	clap clap clap

_____

WHAT WE WANT IS FUN

_____

Challenge

3 Write the chant using new verbs. How many different verbs can you use?
Think about your choice of word **and** your handwriting presentation.

The Poetry United Chant

WHAT DO WE _____   clap clap clap
WHAT DO WE _____   clap clap clap
WHAT DO WE _____   clap clap clap
_____ US A   P   clap clap clap
_____ US AN   O   clap clap clap
_____ US AN   E   clap clap clap
_____ US A   T   clap clap clap
_____ US AN   R   clap clap clap
_____ US A   Y   clap clap clap
_____ US THE RHYTHM ... P O E T R Y
WHAT WE _____ IS POETRY

            clap clap clap
            clap clap clap
            clap clap clap
            YES!

> 3.3 Sound words

Focus

1 a Look at the poem on the next page. Fill in the gaps with difficult
words. You may need to use some words more than once.

   b Underline the sound words.

   lullaby   to   words   like   or   murmur

Words _____ clacker and _____ clack

_____ trains that travel on a track.

_____ to soothe, _____ to sigh

to shush and hush and _____ .

Words to tickle _____ to tease

to _____ , hum or buzz like bees.

Practice

2 Read this section from *Words to Whisper*, by Michaela Morgan.
Answer the questions.

> Cruel words that taint and taunt.
> Eerie words that howl and haunt.
> Words with rhythm. Words with rhyme.
> Words to make you feel just fine.

a What is a cruel word? _____

b What is an eerie word? _____

c Write a list of words that make you feel 'just fine'.

Challenge

3   Write sound words for each letter of the word WORDPOWER.

W   *Wow!   Woo hoo!   whisper   whine*

O   _____

R   _____

D   _____

P   _____

O   _____

W   _____

E   _____

R   _____

> 3.4 Reading a rhyming story poem

Language focus

We can use the word '**for**' to explain the purpose of something.
*Boots **for** muddy places.*

We can use the word '**with**' to explain an extra detail.
*Shoes **with** grown-up laces.*

Focus

1   Draw what shoes or footwear you need for these activities.

a   skiing   b   ballet   c   football

Practice

2   Complete each sentence with *with* or *for*.

a   We have shoes _____ buttons and _____ bows.

b   The salesman says, "What do you need them _____ ?"

c   I sell shoes _____ buckles, shoes _____ pearls.

d   I sell shoes _____ driving, shoes _____ diving, shoes _____ leaving and arriving.

e   I sell shoes _____ funny faces.

Challenge

3   Read the sentences from part 1 of *New Shoes*.

Rewrite each sentence with the correct punctuation.
Do you need to add any of these?

speech marks " "   question mark ?   full stop .   capital letter A

a   I say to the salesman, I need new shoes.

_____

b   He says, What do you need them for

_____

c   i sell shoes with funny faces

_____

d   One shoe, two shoes, I need new shoes!

_____

e   I say to the saleslady, I need new shoes

_____

> 3.5 Planning and writing a rhyming story poem

Focus

1 Fill in the gaps with rhyming words. Use these words to help you.

> pair   trees   lose   springs   please   keys   rings

1 You need shoes with dragon's **wings**,

   a With laces made from fairy _____

   b And soles made of magic _____ ,

2 Shoes for stepping over **seas**,

   c Shoes for jumping into _____ .

   d Shoes with special clockwork _____ .

   e To play where I _____ ,

3 To run where I **choose**,

   f To race with the wind and never _____ .

4 Wonderful shoes for a child to **wear** ...

   g If you can catch me, I'll buy you a _____ !

Practice

5   Complete the chart.
    Write a rhyming word for each underlined word.

Dragon's wings	Ribbons and bows	High heels	Flashing lights	Fancy flowers	Patterned laces

Challenge

6   Make rhyming word charts.

    a   Write words that rhyme with the word in the middle.

    b   In the third chart write your own word in the middle and then
        add your rhyming words.

    c   Add pictures if you want to.

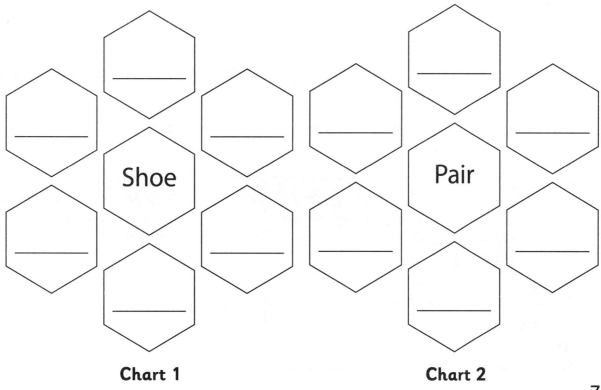

Chart 1   **Chart 2**

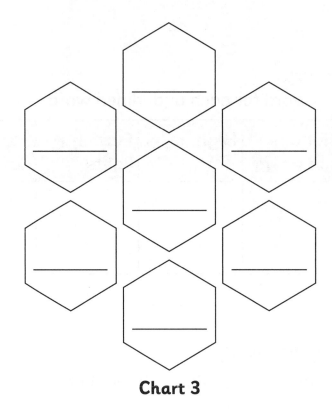

Chart 3

> ## 3.6 Look back

Focus

1 Choose a piece of your own poetry writing from this unit.

 a Re-read your poem to check for mistakes, to see what is good and what you can improve.

 b Ask a partner to read the same poem. Then ask for their feedback. Fill in the chart.

	What is good?	Why is it good?	What can you improve?
What you think			
What others think			

Practice

2 Find a poem that you enjoy. It should have a pattern in the way it sounds. Look at home, in the school library or online.

Write it here. If it is very long, just write a small part of it.

a What pattern does the poem have?

_____

b Why did you choose it?

_____

c Circle or <u>underline</u> the parts of the poem you could use in your own writing.

Challenge

3 Read this short poem. Then answer the questions.

My Shoes

My shoes are new and squeaky shoes,   I liked my old brown leaky shoes

They're very shiny, creaky shoes.   Much better than these creaky shoes –

I wish I had my leaky shoes   These shiny, creaky, squeaky shoes

That mum threw away.   I've got to wear today.

Anon

a List the sound words:

_____

b List the rhyming words:

_____

c List the words that begin with the same letter sound:

_____

d List all the words ending in letter y with sound ee:

_____

e Write another word that rhymes with shiny:

_____

f List the words that have opposite meanings:

_____

4 Long, long ago

> 4.1 Exploring words

> **Language focus**
>
> Words that help us to describe nouns in a more accurate or interesting way are called **adjectives**. In stories we can use adjectives to describe characters and settings.

Focus

1 Draw a picture in each box to match the description.

a A tiny lizard	b A pygmy hippo

c A small turtle <u>with a patterned shell</u> _____ _____	d A little mouse deer _____ _____

2 Circle four words in the table that mean 'small'.

Practice

3 Add extra information to each of the descriptions above.
An example has been done for you.

Challenge

4 Write a description of these small animals using adjectives.

a _____

_____

b _____

_____

_____

b Tarsius monkey

a Shetland pony

> 4.2 Reading and understanding

Focus

1 Read this part of the text.

a Later that day, Tiger saw Sang Kancil standing beside a tree. Tiger's Belly rumbled. 'I won't be tricked this time,' he said to himself. 'Hello Tiger,' said Sang Kancil. 'What are you doing here?' Tiger **grinned**. 'I'm going to eat you for my lunch.'	b Sang Kancil thought quickly. He glanced up at the tree and spotted a bee's nest. He smiled slyly. 'Oh, you can't eat me,' he said. 'Why not?' demanded Tiger. 'Because the king has asked me to look after his drum.'
c 'The king's drum? I'd like to bang that,' said Tiger. Sang Kancil shook his head. 'You can't.' Tiger bared his sharp teeth. 'I think I can,' he growled.	d 'OK, I'll let you,' said Sang Kancil. 'But first, let me escape into the jungle so the King's men don't catch me.' Tiger agreed and reached up to bang the king's drum. Sang Kancil escaped into the jungle. 'Help! Ouch! This isn't a drum,' said Tiger. 'It is a bee's nest and I've been tricked again!'

2 Find these words in the text and circle them.

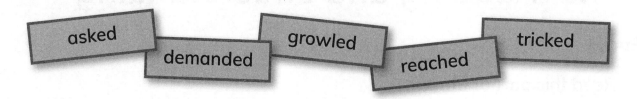

Practice

3 Find these words in the text in their past tense form.

a <u>Underline</u> them.

b Write the past tense form.

c Say what you have to do to write each verb in its past tense form.
An example has been done for you.

Verb in present tense	Verb in past tense	How to form the past tense for this word
grin	grinned	add –ned
glance		
agree		
spot		
smile		
escape		
rumble		
bare		

Challenge

4   Look back at the text. Find these words in their past tense form.

    a Underline them.   b Write the past tense form.

Verb in present tense	Verb in past tense
see	
shake	
say	

> 4.3 Retelling a story

Focus

1   Write in order what Sang Kancil told Tiger.

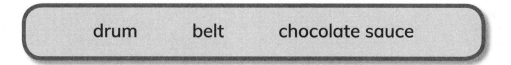

drum   belt   chocolate sauce

    a The king has asked me to look after his _____ .

    b The king has asked me to look after his _____ .

    c The king has asked me to look after his _____ .

Practice

2   Write a sentence for each picture.
    Introduce Sang Kancil and then explain each trick.

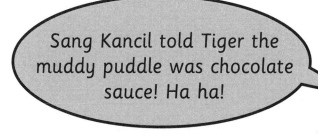

Sang Kancil told Tiger the muddy puddle was chocolate sauce! Ha ha!

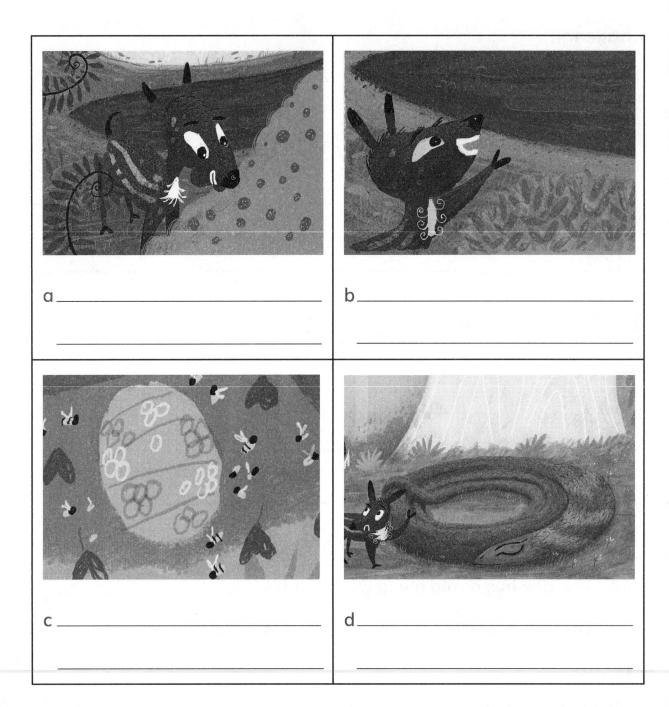

a _____

_____

b _____

_____

c _____

_____

d _____

_____

Challenge

3   Choose one more thing that Sang Kancil could choose to trick Tiger.

_____

_____

> 4.4 Using adjectives to add description to characters and settings

Language focus

Adding adjectives to nouns and noun phrases makes sentences more interesting. Look how this sentence grows with description:

the monster

the monster's hair

the monster's hair is thick

The monster's hair is thick like a bear's.

The monster's hair is thick and white like snow.

Focus

1   How is the monster – *The Abominable Snowman* – described?
    Complete these sentences.

    a   The monster's hair is _____ like a bear's hair.

    b   The monster's hair is _____ like snow.

Practice

2   Choose the right endings for each starter. Draw a line to match them.

Starter	End
Busy like a	ox.
Solid like a	tortoise.
Strong like an	bee.
Slow like a	rock.

Challenge

3   Look again at the chart above.
    Now write two new comparisons from your language.

    a   _____

    b   _____

> 4.5 Exploring a story in chapters

Focus

1   Draw what you think the monster looks like in his cave.

Label parts of his body.

Example: *sharp teeth*

Practice

2   List these chapter headings in the right order to tell the story of *The Abominable Snowman*.

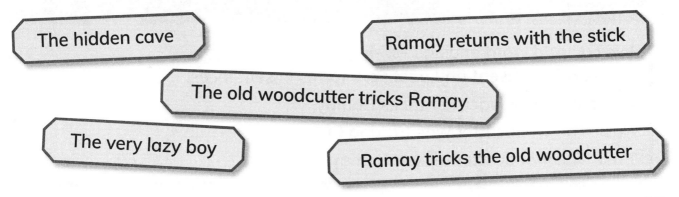

The hidden cave

Ramay returns with the stick

The old woodcutter tricks Ramay

The very lazy boy

Ramay tricks the old woodcutter

Chapter 1: _____

Chapter 2: _____

Chapter 3: _____

Chapter 4: _____

Chapter 5: _____

Challenge

3 Write new chapter headings for this story.

Chapter 1: _____

Chapter 2: _____

Chapter 3: _____

Chapter 4: _____

Chapter 5: _____

> 4.6 Reading aloud and checking understanding

Language focus

We can add word endings –s, –ing
and –ed for present and past verb forms in sentences.
Present: The woodcutter trick**s** Ramay.
Past: The woodcutter was trick**ing** Ramay.
Past: The woodcutter trick**ed** Ramay.

Focus

1   Sort the words into three sets.

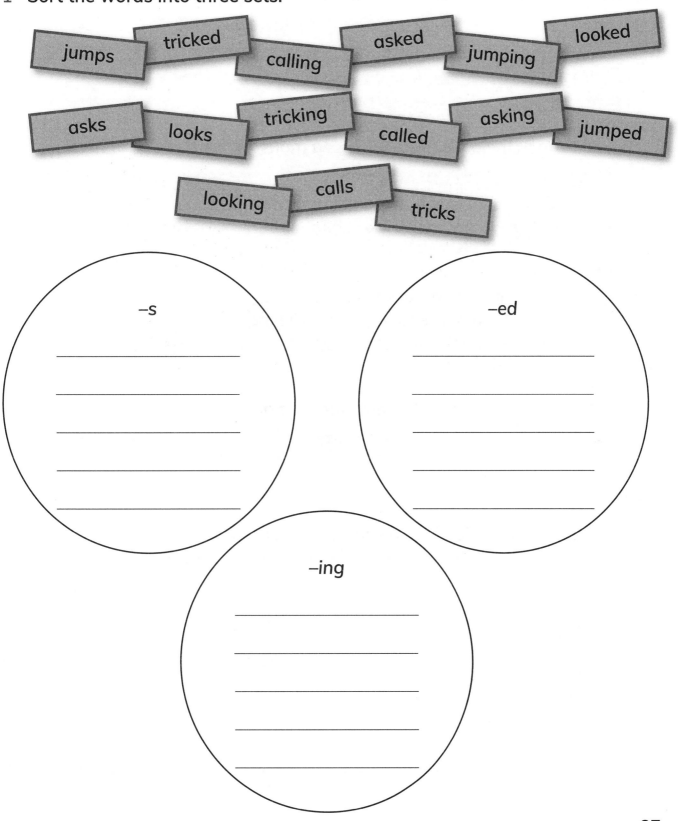

jumps   tricked   calling   asked   jumping   looked

asks   looks   tricking   called   asking   jumped

looking   calls   tricks

–s

_____

_____

_____

_____

–ed

_____

_____

_____

_____

–ing

_____

_____

_____

_____

_____

Practice

2 Read these sentences. Write the correct verb form in the gap.

a Ramay _____ home to look for work.   leaves or leaving?

b Under the roots of the tree was a cave
   and in the cave _____ a monster.   lives or lived?

c Ramay _____ the old woodcutter,
   but the woodcutter tricked him.   tricking or tricked?

d That night when Ramay is _____ ,
   the old woodcutter swaps the wishing
   stick for an old piece of wood.   sleeping or sleeps?

e Now Ramay and the monster are both
   _____ happily ever after.   living or lived?

Challenge

3 Now write a question like this for a partner to do.

> 4.7 Planning and writing a new story ending

> **Language focus**
>
> We can sometimes **join sentences together** using words like *because, if, when, and, but* and *so*.
> Under the roots of the tree was a cave. In the cave lived a monster.
> Under the roots of the tree was a cave and in the cave lived a monster.

Focus

1 Tick (✓) the words you can use to join two sentences together.

- [ ] and
- [ ] when
- [ ] because
- [ ] but
- [ ] so

- [ ] first
- [ ] character
- [ ] setting
- [ ] tricked
- [ ] if

Practice

2 Read these sentences.
   Tick (✓) if they are true and put a cross (✗) if they are untrue.

a You can join sentences with the word *but*. [ ]

b You can join sentences with the word *the*. [ ]

c You can complete this sentence with the word *because*.

   I like traditional stories _____ they are quite funny. [ ]

Challenge

3 Fill the gaps with the best word to join the sentences.

   a Ramay was lazy _____ his mother sent
      him away.

   b The monster was scared _____ he heard
      Ramay chatting to himself.

   c Ramay went home _____ he thought
      he had a magic wishing stick.

> 'Untrue' and 'false' mean the same thing. They are two words with the same meaning.

> 4.8 Story beginnings

Focus

1 Find up to six traditional stories in your library or online that have different story beginnings.

   a Write them here:

   _____

   _____

   _____

_____

_____

_____

b <u>Underline</u> the ones you will try to use in your own writing.

Practice

2 Choose and write the best words for these sentences from the beginning of *Yoshi the Stonecutter*.

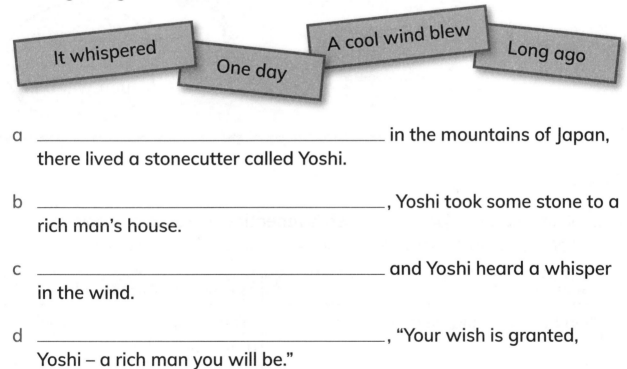

a _____ in the mountains of Japan, there lived a stonecutter called Yoshi.

b _____ , Yoshi took some stone to a rich man's house.

c _____ and Yoshi heard a whisper in the wind.

d _____ , "Your wish is granted, Yoshi – a rich man you will be."

Challenge

3 Finish each sentence to begin a traditional story. Choose words to make the reader want to know more.

a Long ago _____ .

b Once upon a time _____ .

〉 4.9 Exploring the text

Language focus

Language patterns can give us clues about what might happen next in a text. They can help us to continue the story.

Oh I wish I could be ...

Your wish is granted. A ... you will be.

Focus

1   Look at the chart. <u>Underline</u> Yoshi's repeating words in one colour. <u>Underline</u> the Whisper's repeating words in a different colour.

Yoshi	The whisper in the wind
"Oh I wish I could be a rich man,"	"Your wish is granted, Yoshi – a rich man you will be."
"A prince is more powerful than a rich man. Oh I wish I could be a prince,"	"Your wish is granted, Yoshi – a prince you will be."
"The sun is more powerful than a prince. Oh I wish I could be the sun,"	"Your wish is granted, Yoshi – the sun you will be."
"A cloud is more powerful than the sun. Oh I wish I could be a cloud,"	"Your wish is granted, Yoshi – a cloud you will be."

Language focus

Remember, **speech marks** show when someone starts and stops speaking.

"I am rich!" said Yoshi.

"I wish I could be rich," said Yoshi.

Practice

2   Look at the chart. Add the speech marks to the sentences
    in the boxes. An example has been done for you.

Yoshi speech	Rewrite sentence correctly with speech marks
Oh I wish I could be a rich man said Yoshi.	"Oh I wish I could be a rich man," said Yoshi.
Oh I wish I could be a prince said Yoshi.	
Yoshi said the sun is more powerful than a prince!	
Is a cloud more powerful than the sun? asked Yoshi.	

Challenge

3 Look at one of your story books that has speech marks in it.
   Read some of the story to your partner.
   Show in your reading that you notice the speech marks.

4 Ask your partner what you can do to make your reading aloud
   even better. Write it here and practise.

_____

_____

> 4.10 Story endings

Language focus

We use the **past tense** to describe something that happened earlier
or a long time ago.

Focus

1 Add –ed to each verb to change it into the past tense.

a grant _____   d turn _____

b wish _____   e sort _____

c walk _____   f play _____

2   Write a sentence in the past tense using one of the words from Activity 1.

_____

_____

Practice

3   Change each sentence into the past tense by rewriting the underlined word. An example has been done for you.

Long ago in the mountains of Japan, there <u>lives</u> a stonecutter called Yoshi.

Long ago in the mountains of Japan, there <u>lived</u> a stonecutter called Yoshi.

a   Yoshi <u>wants</u> to be a stonecutter.

_____

b   The whisper in the wind <u>smiles</u> at Yoshi.

_____

c   The whisper in the wind <u>grants</u> Yoshi all his wishes.

_____

_____

d   **Yoshi** the stonecutter <u>picks</u> up his tools and <u>starts</u> to work.

_____

_____

Challenge

4 Rewrite each of your past tense sentences from Activity 3. This time, use a different verb in the past tense, but keep the same meaning.

Long ago in the mountains of Japan, there <u>was</u> a stonecutter called Yoshi.

a _____

b _____

c _____

_____

d _____

_____

> 4.11 Planning and writing a circular story

Focus

1 Read all these words. In each line, one word is the odd one out. Circle the odd one out.

a	sun	cloud	tree
b	Yoshi	Japan	Kancil
c	wish	stone	want
d	greedy	poor	sun
e	powerful	helpful	strongest

Practice

2 Read all these words. In each line, one word is the odd one out.
   Circle that word. Take turns with a partner to say why the words
   you chose are odd.

   a grey   granted   Yoshi   great
   b yelled   whispered   grumbled   rains
   c cried   replied   said   tried
   d whisper   rock   white   wish
   e lazy   unhappy   bored   stonecutter

Challenge

3 Make up an 'odd one out' challenge for your partner to complete.

   Write five questions for your challenge (like the ones in Activity 2 above).
   Make sure you know the answers before your partner tries the
   challenge. (You could write them somewhere private.)

   _____

   _____

   _____

   _____

> 4.12 Look back

Focus

1 Choose a piece of your own traditional tale writing.

   a Re-read your writing to check for mistakes, to see what is good
      and what you can improve.

b Fill in this chart.

What is good?	Why is it good?	What can you improve?

Practice

2 a Ask a partner to read the same piece of writing and ask for their feedback. Fill in this chart.

What is good?	Why is it good?	What can you improve?

b Highlight what you will try to use next time.

Challenge

3 a Find a traditional story you would like to read.
Look at home, in the school library or online.

b Draw a picture of it here and say why you want to read it.
How might it help you to improve your own reading and writing?

5 ▶ Computers and robots

〉 5.1 What are computers?

Read this information about computers. Then answer the questions.

How many computers do you have in your house? There may be more than you think.

Desktop computers, laptops and tablets

You have seen these computers. You will see people working or playing on them.

Games consoles

Games consoles are machines that are built for playing games. They are also computers because they are machines that can work with information and solve problems. Many games consoles are connected to the internet.

Smart phones and smart watches

Smart phones contain computers. People use smart phones to talk to people and to text. They also use them to connect to the internet, to play games and to watch videos. Some people wear smart watches that will tell them if they have had enough exercise, or if their phone is ringing, or remind them of things they need to do.

Focus

1 What **two** things does the text tell you about games consoles? Tick (✓) them.

   a Everyone plays computer games. ☐

   b Computer games are fun. ☐

   c Games consoles are computers. ☐

   d Games consoles can be connected to the internet. ☐

2 What can you can do on a smart phone? Write **one** thing.

   _____

Practice

3 What **two** kinds of computer might you find in your home?

   _____   _____

4 What does the text say a computer is?

   _____

   _____

Challenge

5 Why are games consoles computers?

   _____

   _____

6 What might a smart watch tell you? Write **two** things.

   _____   _____

› 5.2 Computer codes

Focus

1 Read the sentences. Put a full stop or a question mark at the end of each sentence.

    a Computers only do what people tell them to do___

    b Do computers just know what to do___

    c Computer programmes are written in code___

    d How can a train teach children to code___

Practice

2 Read about the coding train.

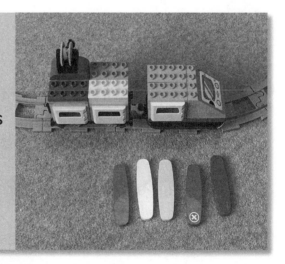

this toy train teaches young children about computer codes after they have built the railway, children can put the coloured 'action bricks' between the rails the train has a little computer inside it and a tiny camera, called a 'sensor', underneath it the computer does what the code tells it to do

    a Add:

       4 full stops   ☐ ☐ ☐ ☐

       4 capital letters   ☐ ☐ ☐ ☐

    b Tick (✓) the boxes when you have added a full stop or a capital letter.

Challenge

3   Write two questions about the coding train for your partner to answer.

Example: *What does the train teach young children?*

Question 1: _____

_____

Question 2: _____

_____

> 5.3 Describing computers

Focus

1   a   <u>Underline</u> all the adjectives in these sentences.
Sometimes, there is more than one adjective in a sentence.

- The digital clock is by the bed.

- Some numbers are red.

- All the numbers are easy to read.

b   Write your own sentence using one of these adjectives.

_____

_____

Practice

> **Language focus**
>
> In English, we join together nouns and adjectives in two ways.
>
> 1   The adjective is often written before the noun:
>
>   some <u>new</u> phones   lots of <u>good</u> games   a <u>clever</u> toy
>
> 2   Sometimes, we write the adjective later in the sentence, after verbs like *is, are, was, were*:
>
>   The phones were <u>new</u>.   The games are <u>good</u>.   The toy is <u>clever</u>.

2   a   Draw lines to join the adjectives to what they tell you about the noun they are describing.

loud, soft, musical	what it is made of
long, tiny, huge	what it sounds like
metal, glass, plastic	how it makes me feel
happy, excited, bored	how big it is

b   Choose two of the adjectives. Use them in sentences.

_____

_____

_____

_____

Challenge

3   Circle the adjectives that tell you about how many of something there are.

> On many digital clocks each number is shown using light bars. Behind every number there are seven light bars. When the number changes, some of the light bars disappear and others appear to show the new digit. Only one digit uses all seven of the light bars. Most calculators use light bars to show numbers too.

4   Write two sentences using adjectives that tell you how many of something there are.

Sentence 1: _____

_____

Sentence 2: _____

_____

> 5.4 Finding information

Language focus

A sentence starts with a capital letter and ends with a full stop or question mark.

Sometimes, we can join sentences together using connectives like *and, but, so, because, if, when.*

Focus

1 Read about computer games.

> There are lots of different kinds of computer games and lots of different machines to play them on. In most computer games, you have to solve a problem because that makes people keep playing. The problem could be finding something, doing a task or winning a race. Players like to win points if they find what they are looking for but they don't like games that are too easy.
>
> You need to teach the computer to follow a series of instructions when you write a computer game because the instructions need to tell the computer what the character can or cannot do. They make the rules for the game so that the player can win points.

a Circle the connectives in the text that are used to join sentences. Sometimes, three sentences are joined together to make one longer sentence.

b Write a list of all the connectives you found.

c   Now write the list of connectives in alphabetical order.

a b c d e f g h i j k l m n o p q r s t u v w x y z

Practice

2   Write a different connective to join each pair of sentences.

a   The computer uses the instructions _____ it knows when to give the player a point.

b   Players must keep playing the game _____ they want to get better at it.

c   Players stop playing a game _____ they have found everything.

Challenge

3   Use a word from the box to begin each of the sentences.

After   Before   First

a   _____ computer programmers write any code they have to decide what the computer will need to be able to do.

b   _____ they write instructions for the computer.

c   _____ they have written the instructions, they can begin to write code.

> 5.5 Introducing robots

Focus

1 Read about robots.

> A robot is a machine controlled by a computer. You can program a robot to do some of the same things that some people do. Robots can make things. They can also go to a dangerous place, like into space, while people stay safe on the ground.

Circle five words in the text where the final 'e' makes a short vowel into a long vowel.

Practice

2 In each line, there is one word where the underlined letter or letters makes a different vowel sound. Circle the word that doesn't match.

d<u>a</u>nger	m<u>a</u>ke	m<u>a</u>ny	s<u>a</u>fe
br<u>ea</u>the	d<u>ee</u>p	n<u>ee</u>d	oc<u>ea</u>ns
mach<u>i</u>ne	n<u>igh</u>t	t<u>i</u>red	unl<u>i</u>ke

Challenge

3 Draw lines to show the syllables in these words.

Example: c o m/p u t/e r

2 syllable words	3 syllable words	4 syllable words
p e o p l e	h o s p i t a l	i n f o r m a t i o n
b o r i n g	d a n g e r o u s	o p e r a t i o n s

› 5.6 What robots can do

> **Language focus**
>
> **Present tense verbs** end in different ways to show how many people are doing the action.
>
> The verbs are underlined in these sentences.
>
> The robot <u>moves</u>.   The robot <u>talks</u>.
>
> The robots <u>move</u>.   The robots <u>talk</u>.
>
> What do you notice about when verbs end with –s?

Focus

1 Write a verb from the box to finish each sentence.

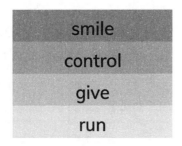 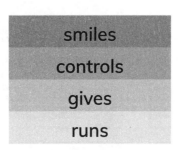

smile	smiles
control	controls
give	gives
run	runs

  a The robot _____ on wheels.

  b People _____ at the robot.

  c Computers _____ robots.

  d The robot _____ people information.

Practice

2 a Write a verb with or without –s in the table. Use these words:

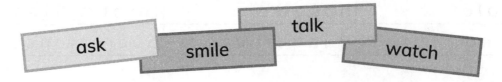

ask   smile   talk   watch

The robot ...	The robots ...
asks	ask

b   Choose two of the –s verbs. Write a sentence for each of them.

Sentence 1: _____

_____

Sentence 2: _____

_____

Challenge

3   Rewrite the sentences to make them about one robot.

Robots do many jobs in my house.	
They cook my meals.	
They clean the floor.	
Robots even cut the grass outside.	

> 5.7 Design a robot

Read the text about the Pepper robot. Then answer the questions.

Sometimes, robots look like people. Pepper is a friendly robot that looks like a person.

Pepper is a robot that talks to people and helps them. Pepper robots work in busy places like restaurants, hotels, airports, stations, offices and shopping malls. The tablet computer on Pepper's chest gives information.

The Pepper robot doesn't have all the senses you have, but it has sensors to help it to find out about the world around it. It doesn't need to taste or smell, but it does need to see, hear, touch things and balance.

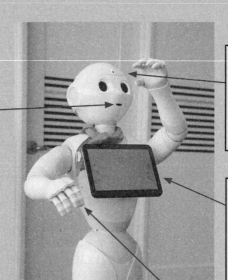

Microphones so the robot can speak when you ask it a question.

Cameras so the robot can 'see' around it and can tell how you are feeling.

Hearing sensors because the robot needs to hear and understand questions.

Bumper sensors in its legs so it doesn't bump into things.

Touch sensors on its hands because it might need to hold something.

Wheels in its feet so it can move around.

Focus

1 a Fill in the missing word. Pepper is a robot that looks like a _____ .

  b Write two places Pepper might work.

   First place: _____

   Second place: _____

Practice

2 a Look at the picture. What does the tablet on Pepper's chest do?

  b Write a question you could ask a Pepper robot in a shopping mall.

   _____

   _____

Challenge

3 Write what Pepper uses instead of the senses you have.

You have ...	Pepper robots have ...
eyes to see	
ears to hear	
hands to touch	

> # 5.8 Introducing drones

Focus

1 Read the text.
Draw a line through a sentence that should not be in this part of the text.

> A drone is a robot. Some drones are as big as aeroplanes but some are so small they can fit on your hand. Some drones have wings so they can fly like a plane. Some aeroplanes have four wings. Some drones have rotors so they can fly like a helicopter.
>
> Many drones carry cameras. Smart phones have cameras. The cameras send videos to the controller, so the controller knows where the drone is.

Practice

2 Read the text. Tick (✓) the sentence that shows the main idea for each section.

All drones are controlled by computer. Sometimes the computer is a long way from the drone. When drones fly into dangerous places, the controller can be sitting in a safe place with a computer. Most small drones and toy drones are controlled by a smaller computer which the controller holds in their hands.	Tick the main idea:
	☐ Drones can go to dangerous places.
	☐ The controller doesn't have to be near the drone.
	☐ All drones are controlled by a computer.

Sometimes we use drones for fun. Some people use drones to play games like hide and seek because the camera on the drone can be used to look for things.

Other people join drone clubs. In drone clubs, they might have races to see whose drone is fastest.

Tick the main idea:

☐ Drones can be fun.

☐ Drones carry cameras.

☐ Drones can race.

Challenge

3 Read each paragraph. Then write a sub-heading for it. The sub-heading should tell you about the main idea for the paragraph.

Subheading: _____

_____

Drones help scientists to know more about creatures who live in the oceans. Drones can fly high above the water and follow whales or dolphins as they travel from one place to another. They can also keep a look out for sharks so that people know if it is safe to swim.

Subheading: _____

_____

Whenever people fly drones, they must think about safety. Even very small drones can be dangerous if they are not flown safely.

> 5.9 Flying a drone

Focus

1 Read these sentences.
Write numbers to show the order you would read them in.

a Now I am better at flying my drone, I can make it hover. ☐

b When I was learning to fly my drone it kept crashing. ☐

c When I am very good at flying my drone, I will enter races. ☐

Practice

2 Read these sentences. Write a word or two at the beginning of each sentence to show the order they should be read in.

a _____ , I found it hard to remember everything I had to do to fly my drone safely.

b _____ , I will be able to remember everything I need to do.

c _____ , I find it hard to move my thumbs in different directions.

Challenge

3 Write all the words you can think of that can be used at the beginning of a sentence to show the order of events. Group the words that mean nearly the same thing, in the same box.

First	Then	Finally

› 5.10 Talk about using your robot

Speaking tip

When you give a talk, you need to think about your words.
But you also need to think about what your face, your body
and your voice are telling your listeners.

Focus

1 a Draw lines to match the faces to the feelings.

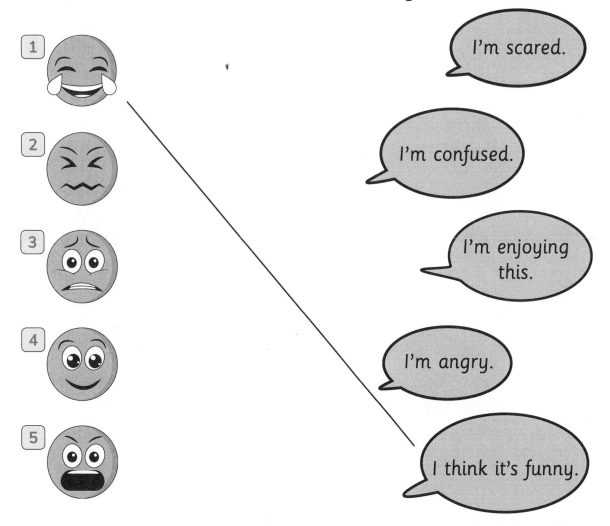

b Circle the face you think is best to use when you're giving a talk.

Practice

2   Your hands, feet and the way you stand give information to your listener.

a   Draw lines to match the body language to the feelings.

b   Circle the body language that you think is best to use when you're giving a talk.

Challenge

3 The way you speak gives information to your listener. Are these good or bad ways of speaking? Draw a line from each verb to where you think it should sit on the scale.

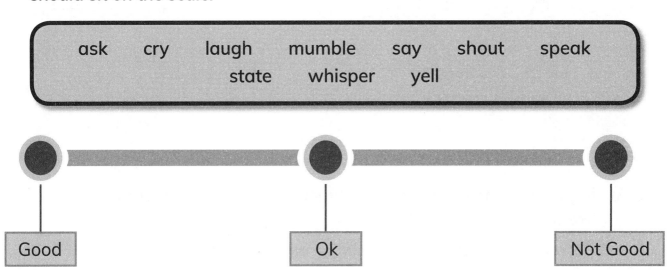

ask   cry   laugh   mumble   say   shout   speak
state   whisper   yell

Good   Ok   Not Good

> 5.11 Writing an explanation

Read this text about a goalkeeper robot.

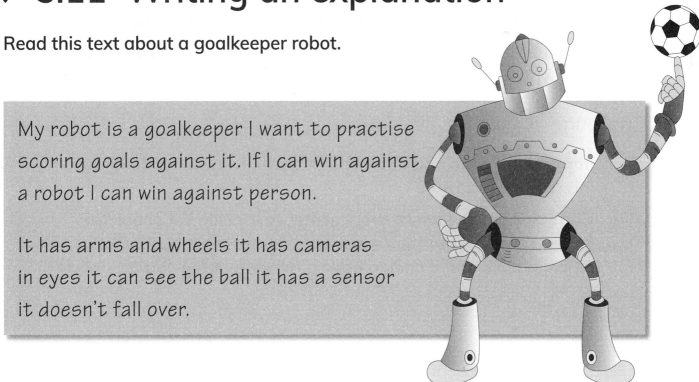

My robot is a goalkeeper I want to practise scoring goals against it. If I can win against a robot I can win against person.

It has arms and wheels it has cameras in eyes it can see the ball it has a sensor it doesn't fall over.

> I wrote instructions I wrote kick the ball throw the ball catch the ball I want it to dive and catch the ball.
>
> _____
>
> _____
>
> _____

Focus

1 a **Improve the text:** join **two** sentences together using words like and, because, when, but, so.

  b **Correct the text:** find **three** places where there should be punctuation and write it in.

Practice

2 a **Improve the text:** add **two** adjectives (describing words).

  b **Correct the text:** find **two places** where there is a missing word and write it in.

Challenge

3 a **Improve the text:** add another sentence giving some detail to interest the reader.

  b **Correct the text:** look at every sentence. Decide if it should be joined to another sentence, using words like and, because, when, but, so or if it should have a full stop at the end.

> 5.12 Look back

Look at all the text in this unit about learning to use a robot.

Focus

1 Make a list of the five most important words about computers and robots that you learned in the unit.

Word 1: _____   Word 4: _____

Word 2: _____   Word 5: _____

Word 3: _____

Practice

2 Use each of the five words in a sentence.

Word 1: _____

_____

Word 2: _____

_____

Word 3: _____

_____

Word 4: _____

_____

Word 5: _____

_____

Challenge

3 Write what each word means.

Word 1 means: _____

_____

Word 2 means: _____

_____

Word 3 means: _____

_____

Word 4 means: _____

_____

Word 5 means: _____

_____

6 On a journey

> 6.1 Word play

Focus

1 Fill in the gaps with these words.

> down   over   out   in

a Pop _____ for a walk.

b Pop _____ to the shop.

c Pop _____ for tea.

d Pop _____ the road.

All of the missing words are about place and direction.

Practice

2 Read the poem. It is not the whole poem, just part of it.
Then fill in the gaps. Use each of these words once:

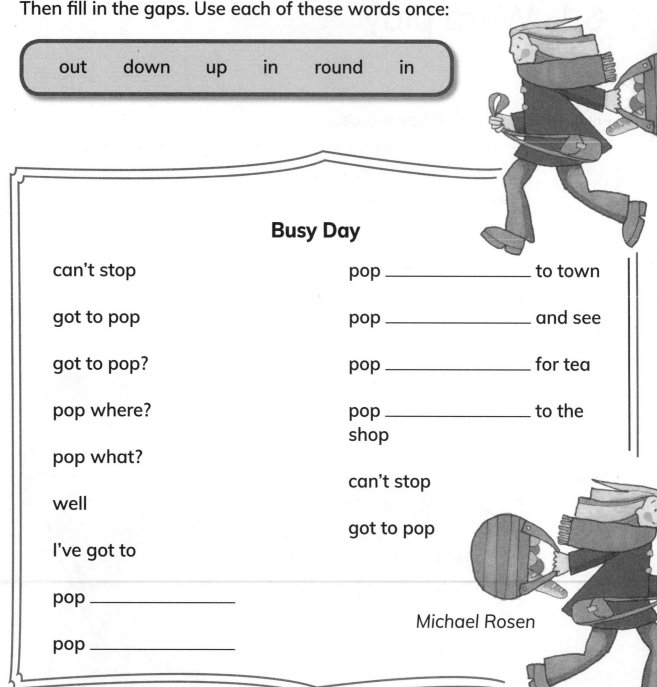

out   down   up   in   round   in

Busy Day

can't stop

got to pop

got to pop?

pop where?

pop what?

well

I've got to

pop _____

pop _____

pop _____ to town

pop _____ and see

pop _____ for tea

pop _____ to the
shop

can't stop

got to pop

Michael Rosen

Challenge

3 Copy these three lines from the poem.

   a Add the correct punctuation.

   b Add something about time.

Use your best handwriting.
Join the letters if you can.
An example has been done for you.

can't stop? _can't stop until 3 o'clock?_____

got to pop? _____

pop where? _____

pop what? _____

The poet has not used capital letters at all in this poem, but he has used question marks. Copy them carefully.

> 6.2 Shape play

Focus

1 Read the poems.

   a Draw round each poem to show its shape.

   b Write what each poem is about.

This poem is about: _____

_____

Twinkle, twinkle little star.
How I wonder what you are
up above the world so high,
like a diamond in the sky.

Spurt

Steam, steam

Rumble, rumble, steam…

And then I start… rumble, rumble.

I lie in wait for many years – a lifeless rock.

I am tall, I am loud, I am ancient, oh so ancient – yet proud.

This poem is about: _____

_____

rolling, rolling, rolling until I hit the full stop. I am a ball that goes

This poem is about: _____

_____

Practice

2   Read the poem *Downhill Racer*.

a   Write the missing rhyming words:

slide   side   glide   ease   skis

b   With a coloured pencil, draw a line between the words to show
the shape better.

Downhill Racer

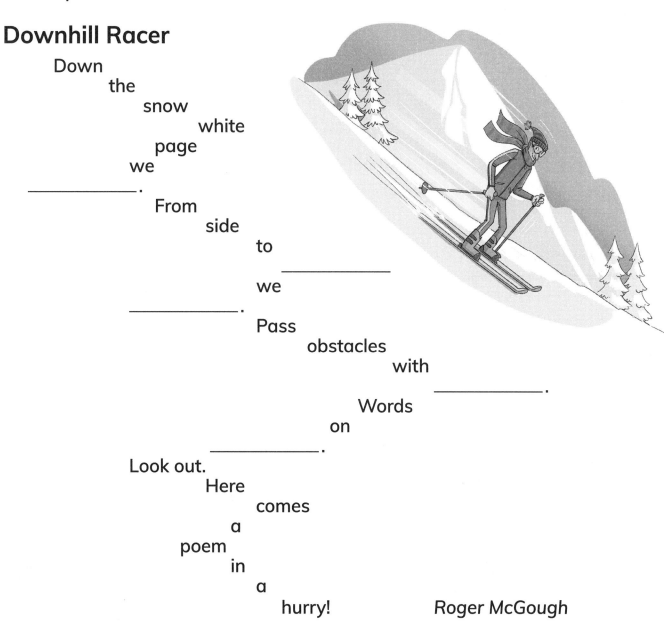

Down
　　the
　　　snow
　　　　white
　　　page
　　we
＿＿＿＿.
　　　From
　　　　side
　　　　　to
　　　　　＿＿＿＿
　　　　　we
＿＿＿＿.
　　　Pass
　　　　obstacles
　　　　　with
　　　　　　＿＿＿＿.
　　　　　Words
　　　　on
　　　　＿＿＿＿.
　　Look out.
　　　Here
　　　　comes
　　　　a
　　poem
　　　in
　　　a
　　　hurry!　　　Roger McGough

Challenge

3 Rewrite the poem *Downhill Racer* making it into a different ski shape.

> 6.3 Repeating a phrase

Focus

1 Write the title of the poem. Then <u>underline</u> the phrase
'Riding down to Boxland' every time you read it.

Title: _____

Riding down to Boxland

where people live in boxes,

Riding down to Boxland

the people live in boxes,

no chickens there,

been eaten by the foxes.

Riding down to Boxland

saw a box looking good,

found a box looking good,

wanted to knock on the box

wondered if I should.

Michael Rosen

2 Draw what you think is in the box.

Practice

3 *Riding Down to Boxland* tells a story.

Sort these lines from the poem into the right order to tell the story.
Use numbers **1–5**.

| 1 | Riding down to boxland where people live in boxes, |

| | laid it out at home, for everyone to see |

| | no answer from inside, not a sound from inside |

| | found a box looking good, wanted to knock on the box, |

| | Riding back from boxland the box coming with me, |

Challenge

4 Write two new lines for *Riding Down to Boxland*.
They can go anywhere in the poem.

_____

_____

> 6.4 Repeating a first line and rhyme

Focus

1 Find these words in the part of the poem, *The River*.
Write how many times each appears.

The River's a winder,

Through valley and hill

He twists and he turns,

He just cannot be still.

a	_____
and	_____
the	_____
he	_____

Practice

2 a Draw what sort of person or animal you think *The River* is like.

b Add some notes to explain what sort of person or animal you think it is.

_____

_____

Challenge

3 Read another part of *The River*. Then answer the questions.

> The River's a hoarder,
>
> And he buries down deep
>
> Those little treasures
>
> That he wants to keep.
>
> Valerie Bloom

a What *little treasures* do you think the River likes to keep?

_____

b How does the River bury them *down deep*?

_____

c How does this make the River sound like a character?

_____

> 6.5 Planning and writing a poem with a patterned structure

Focus

1 a Draw a line that joins a picture to its sound word.

  b Try to change some of these words for better sound words.

Ouch!   _____Ow!_____

Wooo, woooo!   _____

Bing bong!   _____

Cheep, cheep!   _____

Nee-nah, nee-nah! _____

c   What sound words do you use for these things in your own language?
Write some here.

_____

_____

Practice

2   Complete the chart. Write a sound word for each topic.

Topic	Sound word
Cracking an egg	
A bee	
Playing a drum	
Jumping in water	
A roller coaster	
A lion	

Challenge

3   Make a sound word chart.

In the middle, write your topic, for example 'Fireworks' or 'Cricket'.

Round the outside, write the sound words you think the topic makes.
Add pictures if you want to.

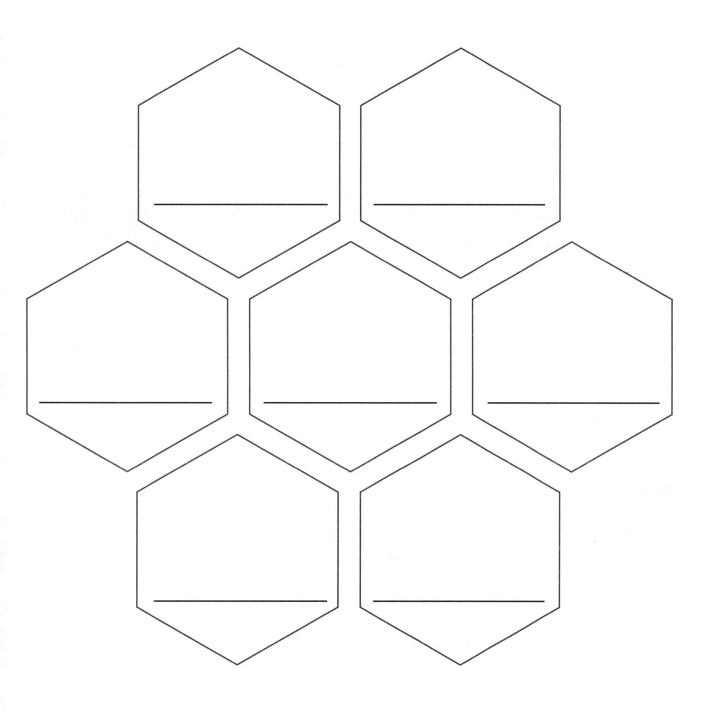

> 6.6 Look back

Focus

1   Choose a piece of your own poetry writing.

Re-read your poem to check for mistakes, to see what is good and what you can improve.

Ask a partner to read the same poem. Then ask for their feedback. Fill in the chart.

	What is good?	Why is it good?	What can you improve?
What you think			
What others think			

Practice

2   Find a poem you enjoy that has a pattern in its structure. Look at home, in the school library or online.

Write it here. You can just write a small part if it is long.

a Describe the poem's pattern: _____

b Say why you chose it: _____

_____

c Circle or <u>underline</u> the parts of the poem you could use in your own writing.

Challenge

3 Read *Exotic Caribbean*.

Exotic Caribbean

Bounce! As the coconuts fall off the palm trees

Tweet, Tweet! Go the newborn, exotic tropical birds

Bang! Go the steel drums at a music festival

Swish! As the waves overlap

Pull! As the fisherman pull in their nets

Sink! Go your feet in the warm, white sand.

Amaal Ali

a Choose one of the words that start each line.

Bounce!   Tweet!   Bang!   Swish!   Pull!   Sink!

b   Write a new poem of just **three lines**. At the beginning of each line, use the word you chose.

Example:

Bounce! As the children fall around.

Bounce! As the ball hits the ground.

Bounce! As I fall into my feather soft bed – and rest my sleepy head.

c   Ask your partner to review your poem.

7 Stories by well-known authors

> 7.1 What do you like to read?

Language focus

When you ask a question, you can do two things:

- Begin with a Wh question word (*What, When, Where, Which, Who, How*).

  Example: *Which book did you like best?*

or

- Begin with a verb like *Do, Have, Are, Can.*
  Example: *Did you like this book?*

Focus

1 Write these statements as questions that begin with a verb.

   a Abeo likes reading adventure stories.

     Does _____?

   b Lotanna started to read a new book.

     _____?

Practice

2 Write questions that begin with a Wh question word about these statements.

    a Ratiq is reading about pirates.

    What _____?

    b Gulmohor likes reading before she goes to sleep.

    _____?

Challenge

3 a Read what Zara says about reading.

I like reading stories about people and things that could really happen. Cao Wenxuan is one of my favourite authors. He writes picture books as well as chapter books. My favourite book is called *Feather*.

    b Write questions you could ask Zara.
      Use these words to start your questions.

      • Have _____?

      • Do _____?

      • Why _____?

      • Which _____?

> 7.2 Introducing voice

Focus

1 Add speech marks to each sentence.

a | Shall | we | play | catch? | asked | Omar.

b | That's | a | good | idea, | said | Pelo.

Practice

2 Write in a verb to show how each character spoke.

Use verbs like: *whispered, called, shouted.*

a 'Throw the ball to me, Beno,' _____ Pelo.

b 'My turn now,' _____ Omar. 'Throw the ball to me.'

Challenge

3 a Add speech marks, full stops, question marks and capital letters.

Beno threw the ball to Omar Omar tried to reach it but Pelo jumped in front of him Omar fell over that's not fair, he complained Beno asked Omar if he was hurt no whispered Omar

Practice reading all of these sentences. Think about how the punctuation helps you to read it well.

> 7.3 Ordering events

Focus

1 Circle the words and phrases that tell you about time passing.

In the morning   Under the table   Behind the house

Gently   That night   Suddenly

Practice

2 Read the text.

> **Sorry Isn't Good Enough, Part 2**
>
> Omar wouldn't talk to Pelo and Pelo didn't understand why. The next day, their friend Zara asked Omar why he was angry.
>
> 'What happened? What made you angry with Pelo?' Zara asked.
>
> 'He pushed me away so that he could get the ball. He pushed me so hard that I fell over,' said Omar. 'He didn't say sorry or anything,' Omar said. 'I don't think friends should be like that.'
>
> After Zara listened, she knew what she must do. She went to find Pelo and told him what Omar had said.
>
> Now Pelo understood why Omar was so angry with him. He was sorry.
>
> 'Then you must tell Omar,' said Zara. 'Here he is!' Zara said and she pulled Pelo towards Omar.

Write words and phrases from the text that tell you about time passing.

Challenge

3 Write four more words and phrases you could use in a story to tell your readers about time passing.

_____   _____

_____   _____

> 7.4 Introducing a text

Focus

1 Ask someone to time you as your read these words as quickly as you can.

went	from	children	just	help
said	have	like	so	do
when	out	what	her	there
don't	old	I'm	by	time
house	about	your	day	made

a Write down how long it took you. _____

How many words did you get wrong? _____

b Read the words again.

How long did it take this time? _____

How many words did you get wrong? _____

Practice

2 Show how you can work out these words by sounding them.
Write one sound in each box.

a round   (r) (ou) (n) (d)

b night

c great

d mother

e before

Challenge

3 Read these words, then tick (✓) the box to show how you worked
each one out.

	I knew the word	I sounded it out	I used syllables	I asked for help
character				
quarrel				
enjoyment				

	I knew the word	I sounded it out	I used syllables	I asked for help
believe				
meaning				

> 7.5 Focus on adjectives

Nouns:	cloth	village	water
Adjectives:	best	clean	colourful

Focus

1 Join each adjective to a noun.
Write one noun phrase and one sentence for each adjective and noun.

Noun or adjective	Noun phrase	Sentence
cloth		
village		
water		
best		
clean		
colourful		

Practice

> **Language focus**
>
> The word endings –y and –ful can be added to some nouns to make them into adjectives.

2 Fill in the table to show the adjectives you can make by adding –y or –ful to these nouns.

Noun	Adjective
help	
luck	
stick	
thought	

Challenge

3 Fill in the boxes to show adjectives that compare.

Adjective	Compared to one other	Compared to all others
small	smaller	smallest
		blackest
slow		
	younger	

> 7.6 Writing an ending for the story

Read this story beginning and then answer the questions.

Aunt Marcella and Uncle Fernando were getting old. Every morning, they sat outside and looked over the peaceful river that flowed by their house. Aunt Marcella said that the water made her feel young inside. Uncle Fernando laughed at her, but he spent most of his time sitting by the river bank trying to catch fish.

One morning, they heard a loud noise on the other side of the river. They saw a line of diggers, concrete mixers, tractors and cranes.

Over the next few days, they watched while the diggers started digging up the ground and more trucks brought bricks and cement.

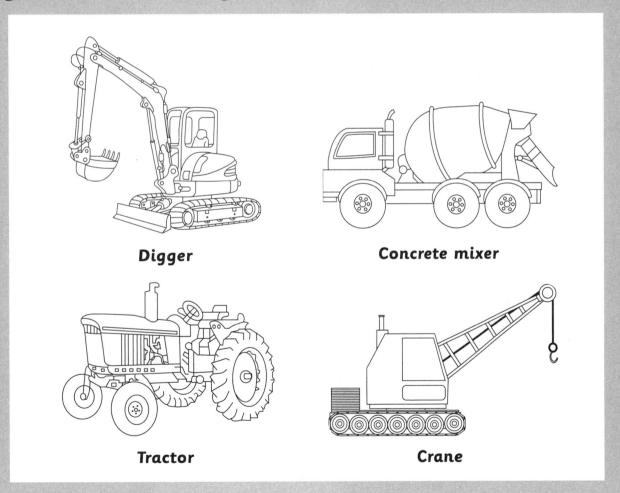

Digger

Concrete mixer

Tractor

Crane

Focus

1 a What did Aunt Marcella and Uncle Fernando do every morning?

_____

_____

b Why did Aunt Marcella like living by the river?

_____

_____

c Why did Uncle Fernandez like living by the river?

_____

_____

Practice

2 a What was making the loud noise?

_____

_____

b Do you think the loud noise is going to be there for a few days or a long time?

_____

_____

c   What do you think might be happening over the river?

_____

_____

Challenge

3   Write three or four sentences about what might happen next in the story.

_____

_____

_____

_____

> 7.7 Introducing a story

Read the story, then complete the activities.

Little Albatross, Part 1

1   Then one bright day Mother and Father Albatross looked at Little Albatross and saw how big he was, and how strong. It would be quite safe, they thought, to leave him for a while and go off fishing together.

2   So away they flew, out over the cliff top, singing again their soaring song, the song of the wandering albatross.

3   They did not see the killer bird beneath them. But the killer bird saw them. He was watching. He was waiting.

4   "Oh Father! Oh Mother!" cried Little Albatross, who had never before been left on his own. "Come back! Come back!"

5   But the wind screamed and the waves roared and they could not hear him. Out over the surging sea they soared, always on the look-out for silver flashing fish swimming below them in the surging sea. One glimpse was all they needed.

Focus

1   Draw lines to join each word from the text to another word with the same meaning.

   a   bright   howled

   b   screamed   sunny

   c   soaring   sight

   d   glimpse   flying

Practice

2   Write one word from the text that tells you:

   a   Mother and Father Albatross saw that

       Little Albatross was growing up _____

   b   the sea was noisy _____

   c   what the fish looked like _____

Challenge

3   Write one word from the text that tells you:

   a   where the albatross nest was _____

   b   how Little Albatross felt when he was alone _____

   c   about the bird that was watching him _____

› 7.8 Language in a story

Focus

1   Draw lines to join the everyday word to the more interesting
    word that sometimes means the same thing.

Everyday word	Interesting word
ate	sobbed
cried	gobbled
slept	snatched
took	dozed

Practice

2   Choose one of the interesting words you wrote above to fill
    in the gap in each sentence.

   a   "Mother, where are you?" _____ the baby bird.

   b   The frightened bird _____ in the cold nest.

   c   The hungry birds greedily _____ up the fish.

   d   The killer bird _____ eggs and baby birds from other nests.

Challenge

3 Read this passage. Find five words you can replace with more interesting words. Circle them, then write them in a list.

> The little bird was alone in the nest. He began to cry because he was hungry and he wanted food. Most of all, he wanted his parents to come back and keep him safe. He knew there were some birds around who might take baby birds from their nests. He was frightened.

————————   ————————

————————   ————————

————————

> 7.9 Story shapes

Read this story. It's called *The Abominable Snowman*.
Then do the activities.

Write **B** to show the ideas at the **beginning** of the story,
M to show ideas in the **middle** and **E** to show ideas at the **end**.

> A long time ago, a boy lived with his mother in the mountains. The boy was called Ramay and he was lazy. Ramay's mother sent him away so that he could find work. He set off alone into the mountains.
>
> All day long, Ramay chatted to himself because he was lonely. The Abominable Snowman lived in a mountain cave and heard Ramay chatting. He listened to what Ramay was saying and imagined the boy to be a monster. Without seeing Ramay, the monster gave him a wishing stick to make him go away and not eat him. Ramay had tricked the monster and was feeling very pleased!

On his way home to his mother, Ramay stayed the night with an old woodcutter. He told the woodcutter about the wishing stick. That night, when Ramay was sleeping, the woodcutter swapped the wishing stick for an old piece of wood. Ramay had no idea the old man had tricked him.

The next morning, Ramay set off home with the old piece of wood.
At home he showed his mother how the wishing stick could grant their wishes, but it didn't work. His mother was angry with him and Ramay blamed the monster. He ran back, but the monster told him it was not his trick, it was the old woodcutter's trick. He gave Ramay a new wishing stick – one that would chase anyone who touched it without permission.

On his way home again, Ramay visited the woodcutter with the new wishing stick. The new stick chased the woodcutter when he tried to steal it in the night. It chased him until Ramay told it to stop.

Ramay returned home with the two wishing sticks. He made wishes for his mother as well as for the kind monster and his family!

Focus

1 Write where these ideas come from?

Where in the story? (B, M or E)	Main event
	Ramay tricked the monster. The monster gave Ramay a wishing stick.
B	Ramay's mother sent him into the mountains.
	Ramay made wishes for the monster.
	The woodcutter tricked Ramay and stole the wishing stick.
	Ramay realised he'd been tricked and the monster gave him a new wishing stick. The woodcutter tried to steal it but it chased him.

Practice

2 Look back at Session 7.3 and the text for *Sorry Isn't Good Enough*.
Write where these ideas are from.

Where in the text? (B, M or E)	Main event
	Omar wouldn't talk to Pelo and Pelo didn't understand why.
	Pelo pushed Omar over and didn't say sorry.
	Zara told Pelo what the problem was.
	Omar forgave Pelo.
	Omar told Zara why he was cross with Pelo.

Challenge

3 Look back at Session 7.4 in the Learner's Book and the introduction to
The Best Tailor in Pinbauê. Write where in the introduction these ideas
are from.

Where in the introduction? (B, M or E)	Main event
	Edinho and his uncle walked beside the murky river.
	The factory was built and changed the village.
	Uncle Flores began to make colourful curtains.
	Uncle Flores was back at his sewing machine.
	Edinho told his uncle he had found colourful materials.

> 7.10 Planning to write a story

Focus

1 a Look at the boxed story of *Little Albatross*.

Little Albatross	Pattern
Mother and Father Albatross left Little Albatross. Killer bird was lurking.	Parents left child. Another animal threatened child.
Mother and Father were caught in fishing net. Killer bird threatened Little Albatross.	Parents couldn't get back. Threatening animal came closer.
Mother and Father escaped and got back in time to scare off killer bird.	Parents managed to get back in time to scare off threatening animal.

b Now look at the storyboard. It tells a story with the same pattern as *Little Albatross*.

Use the storyboard to tell someone a story about *Little Zebra*. Think about the order of the events in the story.

Practice

2 For each picture in the storyboard, write a word or group of words you could use to tell your listener when the events happened. Use words from the box or think of your own words.

Later	Early one morning	One hot day
At last	After that	Eventually
Without warning	Suddenly	When the sun was setting

Picture 1	Picture 2	Picture 3

Challenge

3 Write three interesting words to describe what each character did. Use words from the box or choose your own. If you don't know what the words mean, how can you find out?

attacked	chased	comforted	frightened	galloped	grazed
pounced	prowled	raced	roared	whimpered	worried

a The baby zebra _____ _____ _____

b The adult zebra _____ _____ _____

c The lion _____ _____ _____

4   Now tell the story again, using language of time and some interesting words to describe what the animals did.

a   What was different about your story the second time?

_____

_____

b   What will you try to remember for when you write your own story?

_____

_____

> 7.11 Writing an animal story

Focus

1   Look again at the storyboard of the zebras and lion from Session 7.10. Choose one character in each of the pictures. Write the words they say in the speech bubbles.

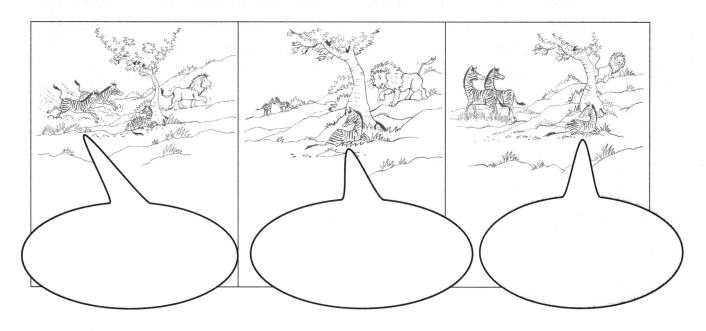

Practice

2 Now write a sentence for each of the pictures, telling us what the animal said and how they said it. Remember to use speech marks.

Sample answer: "We won't be long," smiled Mother Zebra.

Picture 1: _____

_____

Picture 2: _____

_____

Picture 3: _____

_____

Challenge

3 Read this paragraph from the zebra story.
Cross out any sentences that don't belong in the paragraph.

> Mother and Father Zebra were far away looking for food. They were sure no lions would come near their baby. Lions live in Africa. You can sometimes see them in zoos. Then suddenly Mother Zebra heard a distant roar, followed by a whimper from her baby. Baby lions don't have manes. She knew they had to get back as quickly as possible.

> 7.12 Look back

Focus

1 Look at the three pictures of characters from stories in this unit.
Complete the fact file for each one.

Title of story	*Sorry Isn't Good Enough*
Name of author	Lauri Kubuitsile
Main characters	Omar, Pelo, Zara
Setting	School
Type of story	Real life story

Title of story	
Name of author	
Main characters	
Setting	
Type of story	

Title of story	
Name of author	
Main characters	
Setting	
Type of story	

Practice

2   You have only read part of each book. Would you like to read
    more about the characters? Explain why for each book.

Title of story	Sorry Isn't Good Enough		
Would you like to have read more? Explain why	Yes ✓ No ☐ I would like to know if Pelo can keep his promise.	Yes ☐ No ☐	Yes ☐ No ☐

Challenge

3   Write a review of your favourite story from this unit.
    Explain why someone else should read it.

    Begin by saying what you liked about the story.

    _____

    _____

    Then, write a sentence or two explaining what the story is about
    and say how it made you feel.

    _____

    _____

    _____

After that, write something about the vocabulary, or the ideas, or something the writer did that made you like the way they write.

_____

_____

_____

_____

_____

_____

_____

_____

_____

_____

8 ▶ Underwater life

> 8.1 Life under the sea

Language focus

There are two main ways to ask questions in English: questions beginning with a verb, and questions beginning with a Wh question word.

- Questions beginning with a verb (Is, Are, Can, Have, Has, Do, Does) are like statements but with the verb at the front.

Statement	Question
Whales can eat fish.	Can whales eat fish?

  The answers to these questions are usually either 'Yes' or 'No'.

- Questions beginning with a Wh question word (Who, What, When, Where, Why, Which, How) are where you swap a noun phrase in the statement for the Wh question word.

Statement	Whales can eat fish.
Question 1	What can eat fish?
Question 2	What can whales eat?

The answer to these questions will usually be information.

Read about the seabed. Then complete the activities.

The seabed is not flat, at least not in the middle of the oceans. At different places the seabed is covered with sand, with rocks, or with plants like kelp. Near the coast, the seabed is flat or it is has a gentle slope. Deep under the oceans, there are mountains and valleys as well as huge flat areas. The mountains under the sea are all volcanoes. Some are so high that they stick up out of the water and their tops make islands.

Focus

1 Put these words in order to make questions.
  All these questions begin with a Wh word.

  a   volcano?   is   What   a

  _____

  b   seabed   is   Where   the   flat?

  _____

  c   volcanoes   islands?   How   do   make

  _____

Practice

2 Put these words in order to make questions.
  All these questions begin with a verb.

  a   seabed   flat?   Is   the

  _____

  b   under   sea?   there   mountains   the   Are

  _____

  c   sand   seabed?   there   Is   the   on

  _____

  d   all   volcanoes?   Are   mountains   underwater

  _____

Challenge

3 Write three more questions about the seabed.

Question 1: _____

Question 2: _____

Question 3: _____

〉 8.2 Fish and whales

Focus

1 Write the missing vowels to finish the words.

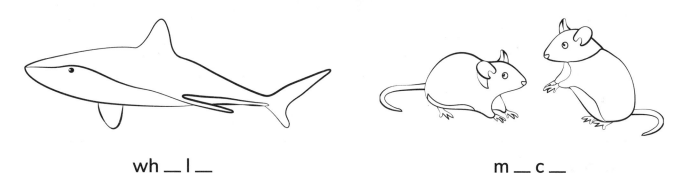

wh _ l _

m _ c _

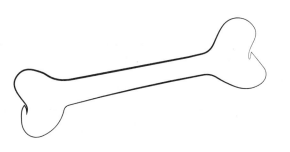

b _ n _

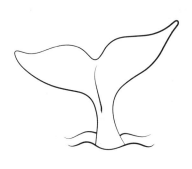

fl _ k _

Practice

2 Write new words that rhyme.

ball   steer   air   blow

_____   _____   _____   _____

Challenge

3 Read the words in the table. They all have some letters that are harder to spell. Write the word and circle the harder bit. How will you remember it?

Write the word twice more.

Word	Write and circle the difficult bit	Write the word again ...	... and again
any	@ny		
every			
many			
most			
some			
all			

› 8.3 More about whales

Focus

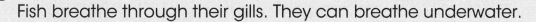

1 Read the sentences.

   a Circle the nouns or noun phrases.

   b <u>Underline</u> the pronouns.

> Fish breathe through their gills. They can breathe underwater.
>
> A fish has scales on its skin. They help to protect it.
>
> Fish have several fins. They use their fins to steer.

Practice

Language focus

A **pronoun** is a word that can take the place of a noun or noun phrase in a sentence.

Words like *it, I, you, they* are pronouns.

2 Look at this text. Draw a circle around each <u>underlined</u> pronoun and join it to the noun phrase it replaces.

An example has been done for you.

> **Whales**
>
> What kind of animal is a whale?
>
> There are many different kinds of whales. Whales spend their lives in the seas and oceans of the world, but **they** are not fish. Whales are mammals so **they** must breathe air.

How do whales breathe?

If a whale cannot reach the surface of the water to breathe, <u>it</u> will drown. A whale's nostrils are called blowholes. <u>They</u> are on top of the whale's head so the whale can breathe when <u>it</u> comes to the surface of the sea. Some whales can hold their breath underwater for more than two hours!

How do whales move?

A whale's tail has two tail flukes. <u>They</u> move up and down to push the whale forwards through the water. Whales use their fins for steering.

Challenge

3   Write pronouns where there are gaps in the text.

Baleen Whales

Baleen whales are big, but _____ eat some of the smallest creatures on earth. _____ have huge plates in their mouths made of baleen. Baleen looks like the teeth in a comb. _____ is made from the same material as _____ fingernails.

› 8.4 Where fish live

Focus

1 Fill in the gaps in these alphabets.

a a b ___ d e f ___ h i j k ___ m n o ___ q r ___ t u v ___ x y z

b a ___ c d e ___ g h ___ j k l m ___ o p q ___ s t ___ v w x ___ z

c a b c ___ e f g ___ i j ___ l m n ___ p ___ r s ___ u ___ w x y ___

d ___ b c d ___ f g h i ___ k l ___ n o p q ___ s t ___ v w ___ y z

Practice

2 Write the words in each line in alphabetical order.

a sea   fish   lake   ocean

_____

b river   seaweed   coral reef   land

_____

c stream   water   dam   rock

_____

Challenge

3 Write the missing words in the glossary. Use the words in the box.

seaweed   coral reef   lake   ocean   river

Glossary

a _____ : an island made out of millions of the shells of tiny creatures called coral.

b _____ : a big pool of water, usually fresh water, that is not part of a sea.

c _____ : a huge amount of salt water. The planet has five enormous ones.

d _____ : plants that grow in the sea.

e _____ : flows into the sea or out of a lake.

4 Write three words from the glossary that you want to remember.

_____   _____

_____

> 8.5 Animals that eat fish

Language focus

Statements usually begin with a noun, noun phrase or a pronoun.

Lots of people like to eat fish.   **We** like to eat fish.

Questions usually begin with a verb or a wh question word.

Do you like to eat fish?   **Which** fish do you like to eat?

Commands begin with a bossy verb or a time sequencing word.

Eat your fish.   **First**, eat your fish.

Change each sentence to a different kind of sentence.

Focus

1 **Statement:** Fish are eaten by other fish.

Question: _____

2 **Statement:** Grizzly bears catch fish in rivers.

Question: _____

3 **Statement:** Polar bears catch fish underwater.

Question: _____

Practice

4 **Question:** Do birds eat fish?

Statement: _____

5 **Question:** Has a fish got fins?

Statement: _____

6 **Question:** Is a shark a fish?

Statement: _____

Challenge

7 **Question:** Can you catch fish?

Command: _____

8 **Question:** Do you like eating fish?

Command: _____

9   **Question:** Have you seen a fish swimming?

   Command: _____

> 8.6 Finding information from charts

Read the text in the chart, then do the activities.

Sea creatures	What kind of animal is it?	What does it eat?	How does it move?	Interesting fact
Great White shark	fish	any animal in the sea	swims with its fins and its tail	A shark will drown if it stops swimming.
Killer whale	mammal	any animal in the sea	swims with its flippers and tail	Killer whales are more like dolphins than sharks.
Emperor penguin	bird	fish	waddles on its feet or slides on its tummy uses its wings as flippers to swim	They can stay underwater for 20 minutes.
Leatherback turtle	reptile	jellyfish	flaps its flippers in the water drags itself on land	leatherbacks can grow over 2 metres (6 feet) long.

Focus

1   Draw lines to match the creatures to how they move.

Great White shark   swims with its flippers

Killer whale   drags itself

Emperor penguin   waddles

Leatherback turtle   swims with its fins

Practice

2   Fill in the gaps in the sentences using information from the chart.

a   _____ eat jellyfish.

b   Penguins eat _____ .

c   _____ eat any large sea animals.

Challenge

3   Fill in the gaps in the text using information from the chart.

The Great White shark is a _____ . It moves quickly through the
water and swims using its _____ . Unlike the shark, the killer
whale is a _____ . It swims with its _____ instead of fins.

The _____ is a reptile. It has flippers too. It swims very well in
water but has to _____ itself on land.

The _____ is a bird. On land, it _____ or _____ .
In the water, it uses its _____ as fins.

> 8.7 Different ways of sharing information

Focus

1 Read the sentences about turtles. <u>Underline</u> the verb in each one.

   a The female turtle crawls onto a beach.

   b She digs a hole in the sand.

   c She is laying her eggs in the hole.

Language focus

The verb tense tells us <u>when</u> something happens.

We use the **present tense** for something that is **happening now**:

Example: *The shark is chasing the fish.*

We also use it for something that *always happens*:

Example: *Sharks chase fish.*

Practice

2 Fill in the gaps with the verb shown.
Make sure you use the right verb ending.

a Turtles _____ most of their time at sea.	spend
b They _____ by flapping their flippers.	move
c A turtle _____ four flippers.	have

Challenge

3 Rewrite each sentence using an –ing verb.

a Some turtles float near the seabed to sleep.

Some turtles <u>are floating</u> on the sea to sleep.

b The turtle lays her eggs in the sand.

_____

c Leatherback turtles eat jellyfish.

_____

d The turtle grows slowly.

_____

› 8.8 Finding information on websites

Focus

1 Look at the words. Circle the letters that make the sound of the vowel.

a r(ee)f   b h a r d   c s h e l l   d s h a p e

e s t a y   f c o r a l   g p o l y p   h c o l o u r

i i s l a n d   j w a t e r

Practice

2 Look at the words. Draw lines to show the syllables.

a i s l a n d   b p o l y p   c o c e a n   d c r e a t u r e s

e m i l l i o n s   f a n i m a l   g t o g e t h e r   h c o l o u r f u l

Challenge

3 Write the words in the correct column to show how many syllables are in each word.

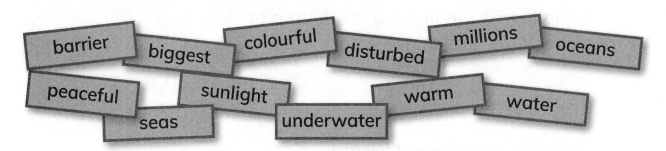

One syllable	Two syllables	Three syllables	Four syllables

> 8.9 Features of report texts

Language focus

Information report texts tell you about what things are like.

Begin by the introduction. After that, you can read the other sections in any order.

Here are some features you may find in an information report text:

- headings and subheadings
- ideas grouped in paragraphs or sections
- noun phrases and adjectives that help you to understand what something looks like
- diagrams, maps, charts or lists
- photographs
- text in the present tense
- sentences that are joined by words such as *and*, *but*, *because*
- a glossary.

Focus

1 Circle all the words in each line that are adjectives.

   a The fish are ...   colourful   quickly   swift   wriggly

   b The shark is ...   grey   graceful   scary   teeth

   c The turtle is ... purposeful scaly   slow   digging

   d The whale is ... hungry   mammal   slowly   wrinkly

Practice

2 <u>Underline</u> the noun phrases in the report text.

Clownfish

Clownfish are found near coral reefs growing in warm water.

Some clownfish are orange and white but others have yellow, red or brown stripes.

Clownfish live near sea anemones and are sometimes called anemone fish. Sea anemones have poisonous tentacles that poison most small fish, but the clownfish have special slime on their skin that protects them.

Challenge

3 Write three noun phrases with adjectives you could use in a report text to describe the fish in the picture.

Phrase 1: _____

Phrase 2: _____

Phrase 3: _____

› 8.10 Planning and writing a report text

Focus

1 Tick (✓) the features you might see in an information report text.

a Glossary: to explain what some words mean ☐

b Subheadings: to tell you what a section is about ☐

c Introduction: to tell you want the text is about ☐

d Instructions: to tell you what to do ☐

e Memories: to tell you what the author enjoyed ☐

f Plans: to tell you what the author might do next ☐

Practice

2 Tick (✓) the sentences you might find in an information report text about reef sharks.

a I love reef sharks. ☐

b Reef sharks are predators and they eat other fish. ☐

c Mario saw a reef shark when he was on holiday in India. ☐

d Reef sharks are so sweet – they the prettiest of all the sharks. ☐

e Reef sharks like shallower water and are often near the surface. ☐

f Diver Dan saw a reef shark. He tried to give it sandwiches to eat. ☐

Challenge

3 Sort these sentences into two groups that are about the same thing.
Underline each group of sentences in a different colour.

> Jellyfish have long tentacles. Jellyfish float in the sea. Jellyfish have soft bodies. Their tentacles are poisonous. Venom pumps through the tentacles and stings fish. Most of a jellyfish is made up of water. Fish that are stung are taken to the mouth to be eaten.

4 Write a subheading for each of your groups of sentences.
Underline each subheading in the same colour as the sentences.

Group 1: _____

Group 2: _____

> 8.11 Improving and correcting a report text

There are three texts in this section. Correct and improve them.
Put a tick (✓) in a box when you have changed something.

Focus

1 Add punctuation to Text 1.

   You will need:

   a full stops ☐☐☐☐

   b capital letters ☐☐☐

   c question marks ☐

1

Sharks

What are sharks

Sharks are fish there are many different kinds of shark they live in all
the oceans of the world some freshwater sharks even live in lakes and rivers

Practice

2 a Find two places where you can add adjectives to Text 2.

b Find two nouns or noun phrases to replace with a pronoun.

c Find one place to join two sentences together.

2

Which senses does a shark use?

Sharks are hunters. Sharks use their senses to hunt.

A shark's best sense is its sense of smell. A shark can smell a drop of blood 400 metres away in the ocean.

Sharks can hear a fish moving in the water even if the fish is too far away for the shark to see.

Some sharks can see as far as 50 metres. Other sharks don't see so well.

Challenge

3 Find three places where you can use a better word or phrase in Text 3.

3

What is inside a shark's mouth?

Sharks are born with two sets of teeth. For all their lives, they always have a row of teeth behind the teeth they use. When a tooth comes out, another tooth goes into its place and a new tooth grows in the row behind it. Sharks' teeth are very good.

Sharks can feel with their teeth. They can bite things to see if they can be eaten.

› 8.12 Look back

Answer the questions about sharks.

Focus

1 Where do sharks live? Tick (✓) all the places mentioned.

   a oceans ☐

   b rivers ☐

   c ponds ☐

   d swimming pools ☐

   e lakes ☐

2 How far away can a shark smell blood? Tick (✓) one.

50 metres ☐

400 metres ☐

500 metres ☐

Practice

3 Why does a shark need good senses?

_____

_____

4 Which is a shark's best sense?

_____

_____

Challenge

5 Why do you think a shark needs so many teeth?

_____

_____

6 Give one reason a shark might bite something.

_____

_____

9 ▶ Creatures everywhere

❯ 9.1 The elephant

Focus

1 Write three words that rhyme with *mice*.

Word 1: _____   Word 2: _____

Word 3: _____

Practice

2 Read the poem. (It goes onto the next page, too.)
Circle the words in each verse that rhyme.

The Bear That Should NOT Be There

There's a bear on my chair.
It shouldn't be there.
I'll give it a glare.
Has it gone?
There's a bear on my chair.
It's eating a pear
And there's juice everywhere.
Has it gone?
I said "GO AWAY BEAR!
I don't want you there!
Go back to your lair!"

Has it gone?
Now I'M in my chair,
And it's sticky with pear
But at least there's no bear.
It has gone.

Challenge

3   Write the rhyming words from the poem so they match the
    spelling pattern.

Spelling pattern	ear	are	air	ere
Words from the poem	bear			

> 9.2 On safari

Focus

1   <u>Underline</u> all the words and phrases that could tell you about a setting.

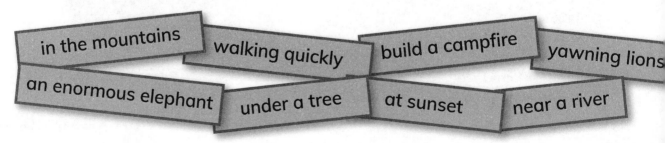

in the mountains   walking quickly   build a campfire   yawning lions

an enormous elephant   under a tree   at sunset   near a river

Practice

2 <u>Underline</u> all the words and phrases that tell you about the setting.

Early one morning, a group of people were walking across the grasslands of Tanzania. They were on their way to a distant village. They could see mountains in the distance but near to them there were empty grasslands and some acacia trees.

Challenge

3 Use words and phrases from Activity 1 to write your own paragraph about the setting.

_____

_____

_____

_____

_____

_____

_____

_____

_____

_____

> 9.3 Rainforest

Language focus

Most verbs have past tenses ending in –ed. Some verbs have different words for past and present tenses, which you need to look out for, for example: *sleep, slept; run, ran; is, was.*

Focus

1   Draw lines to join the verbs to their past tenses.

break	burnt		hear	hit
build	broke		hide	hung
burn	bought		hit	heard
buy	built		hang	hid

Practice

2   Read the verb forms. Write the missing verbs.

Present tense	Past tense
eat	ate
get	
draw	

Present tense	Past tense
	kept
	had
	made

Challenge

3   The verb to be is a particularly difficult verb.

Fill in the table showing different forms of the verb to be.

Pronoun	Simple present tense	Simple past tense
I	am	was
you	are	
He / she / it		was
We / they		were

> 9.4 Crocodiles

Language focus

The letter 'e' at the end of a word often makes a short vowel into a long vowel. This is called a split digraph.

Say these words: tap / tape   bit / bite   hop / hope   tub / tube

Focus

1 Add 'e' to each of these words.
Draw a picture to show the meaning of each new word you make.

Word	man	kit	not	tub
New word				
Picture				

Practice

1 Write a word where the 'e' makes a long vowel that sounds the same as each of these words.

main
m_____

right
wr_____

plain
p_____

road
r_____

eight
a_____

tail
t_____

sail
s_____

rows
r_____

Challenge

3   Use a word with a long vowel ending in 'e' to fill the spaces in these lines.

a   I have a <u>nose</u> in the middle of my <u>*face*</u>

b   I can play a t_____ on my violin.

c   There was sm_____ coming from the fire.

d   I a_____ a big b_____ of my apple.

e   Would you l_____ a sl_____ of pie?

⟩ 9.5 Writing an ode poem

Focus

1   Write the names of the animal body parts underneath the name of the animal.

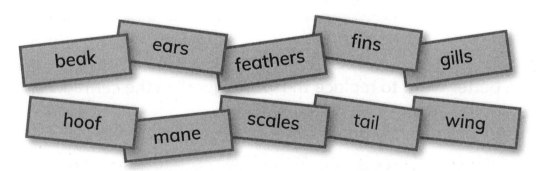

Goose	Horse	Fish

Practice

2 Read the sentences. Circle the words that are closest in meaning to the underlined words.

a The goose <u>went</u> on the water.

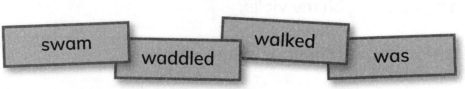

b The goose <u>went</u> on the grass.

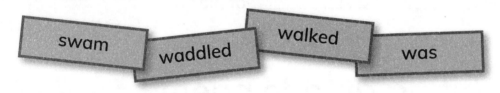

c The goose <u>ate</u> the grass.

Challenge

3 Write a better word to replace the word 'good' in the sentences.

a The goose was very good. _____

b The ice cream was very good. _____

c The child was very good. _____

› 9.6 Look back

Focus

1 Write the alphabet in your best handwriting.

a b c d e f g h i j k l m n o p q r s t u v w x y z

_____

_____

_____

Practice

2 Write the animal names in your best handwriting. Try to join as many letters as possible. Which letters should you *not* join?

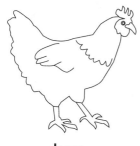

hen

lion

_____

_____

bear

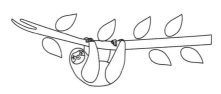

sloth

_____

_____

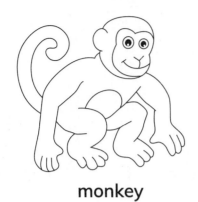

monkey

penguin

_____

_____

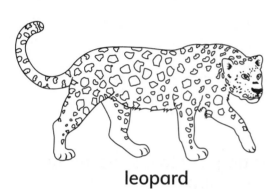

leopard

elephant

_____

_____

Challenge

3 Write the Ode to a Goose in your best handwriting.
   Which letters can you join?

   Goose, goose, goose,
   You bend your neck towards the sky and sing.
   Your white feathers float on the emerald water,
   Your red feet push the clear waves.

   _____

   _____

   _____

   _____